CON
EDINBURGH

TWICE YE

LOST TABOOS

Editorial	3
Fiction	
David Almond: *Buffalo Camel Llama Zebra Ass*	13
Yvonne D. Claire: *Over, All Over and Beyond*	17
R. F. Clerk: *Head*	23
Ian Hunt: *The Daubers*	28
Long Poems	
Graham Fulton: *Normal Appetites*	41
Drew Milne: *Aggropolis*	48
Lost Poets Found	
Andrew Greig: *Horns & Wings & Stabiliser Things*	59
That Summer	72
Brian McCabe: *Appreciations*	74
six poems	80
Ron Butlin: *The Lost Poets*	86
from *Night Visits*	89
The Taboo-Word Totem	
Duncan McLean: *An ABC of Bad Language*	103
Willy Maley: *Swearing Blind*	105
David Stenhouse: *A Wholly Healthy Scotland*	113
Christopher Whyte: *Unspeakable Heterosexuality*	123
Alan Freeman: *Ourselves as Others*	135
Ian Cadman: *two poems*	142
Reviews & Shortleet	149

Edinburgh Review, 22 George Square, Edinburgh EH8 9LF
tel 0131-650 6206
fax 0131-662 0053

editors	Robert Alan Jamieson
	Gavin Wallace
advisory editors	Jackie Jones, Murdo Macdonald
production	Pam O'Connor
publicity	Kathryn MacLean
logo	Alasdair Gray
©	the contributors 1996

ISSN 0267 6672   ISBN 0 7486 0813 3

distributed in the UK by Edinburgh University Press
typeset in Sabon by Koinonia Ltd, Bury
printed and bound in Great Britain by
by Page Bros Limited, Norwich

subsidised by the  THE SCOTTISH ARTS COUNCIL

back issues available
from Polygon,
22 George Square,
Edinburgh EH8 9LF
tel 0131-650 6206

EDITORIAL

Lost Taboos

> ... notwithstanding differences of power, money, race, gender, age and class, there remains one currency common to all of us. There remains one thing that makes possible exchange, shared memory, self-affirmation and collective identity. And isn't that currency known and available to everybody regardless of this or that? And isn't that common currency therefore the basis for a democratic state that will not discriminate between the stronger and the weak? And isn't that indispensable, indiscriminate, or non-discriminating, currency our language? Isn't that so? ...
> ... this is not a democratic state. And we put up with that. We do not have a democratic language. And we put up with that. We have the language of the powerful that perpetuates that power through the censorship of dissenting views.
>
> **June Jordan, from 'Problems of Language in a Democratic State' in** *Moving Towards Home: Political Essays*

The transformation of the public perception of James Kelman, from a writer whose first novel *The Busconductor Hines* was derided as 'written entirely in Glaswegian' at the presentation of the Booker Prize for 1984 by the Chairman of the Judges, Richard Cobb, into the Booker winning author of *How Late It Was, How Late* in 1994, is a triumph for a determined artist over an initially hostile establishment. His ground-breaking work has inspired a younger generation of Scottish writers. Central in this has been the deployment of what has been called 'linguistic realism' to extend literature to include the language and experience of the Scottish working class, not as a series of humorous sketches hinging on the fact that all the characters bar the narrator speak some funny-farm form of non-standard English, nor as a sanitised version for delicate sensibilities, but as literature which is linguistically rooted in the culture it describes. Often this is language which would in the past have been categorised as 'blasphemous', 'bad' or 'dirty', 'the language of the gutter' by certain sections of society.

Not that attitudes have changed entirely – there are still many people who find this new writing distasteful, who criticise it as portraying Scotland in the worst possible light, like a literary parallel to Govan's grossest, Rab C. Nesbitt. One of the fiercest examples of this attitude, one of many published during the post-Booker controversy, is recorded in *The Scots Magazine* for December 1994, where its former editor Maurice Fleming lambasts Kelman and his 'school':

> James Kelman is the leader of the pack with his dreary depictions of life at the bottom end of the social scale in darkest Glasgow. His characters are without hope, without ambition and without any vocabulary other than streams of abuse and vituperation studded with expletives. He has been praised for giving a voice to the inarticulate, but was it really worth doing? If the object of the exercise is to win for his characters a share of our compassion, it doesn't work. We end up hating them as they hate us, the 'haves'.

These are strong words, not at all the warm autumnal glow normally associated with *The Scots Magazine*. 'Hate' is not a word to throw around lightly. Yet Fleming is clearly sure of his audience, sure enough at any rate to appeal to them as 'we', so suggesting a clear division between 'them' and 'us', as if sides must be taken, principles stood by, the battle fought. If 'we' are permitted to conclude that granting speech to the silent in literature is a creative act not 'really worth doing', then by definition this legitimates the view that certain ways of speaking denote thoughts not worth having, or – more disturbingly – lives not worth living. Fleming goes on:

> Kelman stood alone for a time, as the writer who had broken through the language barrier; he used more gutter obscenities than anyone else. Now, others have caught up with him and strive to surpass his total. Irvine Welsh is the new champion, having set out to do for Edinburgh low life what Kelman does for poor old Glasgow ... ... Needless to say, some of the trendy critics have taken Welsh to their hearts as they did Kelman when he started, while hard on the heels of the Terrible Twosome comes one Duncan McLean, desperate to plumb even deeper depths of depravity.

Never mind the factual error (McLean actually preceded Welsh as a published author and was influential in Welsh's emergence) or the hilarious notion that writers are engaged in some kind of 'I can pee higher than you' swearing contest; attitudes such as Fleming propagates should not pass unchallenged. This is a serious cultural issue, more than just another generalised instance of how the avant-garde runs the risk of upsetting the bourgeoisie – this is about how Scottish literature is portrayed, now. After all, Fleming's column is the handiwork of a respected former editor of one of Scotland's popular institutions, 'the world's top-selling Scottish interest title' as it bills itself, with a wide circulation among Scots abroad; that Fleming should attempt to influence the opinion of readers who may not yet have approached (and never will, if he has his way) the writing of the authors named is worrying. In its eagerness to lump together four very different writers (Kelman, McLean, Welsh and later Christopher Rush, who is viewed as something of a traitor for *The Last Lesson of the Afternoon*, having firstly charmed *SM* readers with his East Neuk stories) Fleming's rhetoric is deliberately misleading, supplanting 'sad fact' for what is opinion, merely how things 'appear'.

> The sad fact is that the school of modern writers I have been discussing appear to view Scotland with undisguised and malicious disgust. They see it as a sink of vice and hold not an atom of love or affection for it or for their fellow Scots.

This again is very strong polemic. Fleming holds up Lewis Grassic Gibbon as one exemplar of a writer who managed to deal with the coarseness of life without recourse to 'filthy language':

> I will probably be told that the filthy language used in these and other contemporary novels is essential; because it would be used by the characters depicted. I accept that as a valid argument but still maintain that it should not be necessary.
> Did Gorki find it necessary when he sat down to write his great and moving depiction of the underworld *The Lower Depths*? Did Louis (sic) Grassic Gibbon in his monumental trilogy of working-class folk, *A Scots Quair*?

Clever, but contradictory: Fleming accepts that it may be 'essential' but then refuses to accept it as 'necessary', while his advocacy of Gibbon as a writer who did not offend good taste is at odds with the reception given by many to his books when they appeared in the early thirties.

It may be telling that the voices Fleming objects to are perceived as urban, a long distance away from the largely rural world which *The Scots Magazine* of the 1990s depicts, in its lavishly coloured photos of Scotland's beauties and quaint country tales and travails. This distinction in attitude is pinpointed in *Bad Language* (1990) by Lars Andersson and Peter Trudgill:

> The reaction to rural Scots is often very positive: it is seen as 'good, old Scots speech'. Urban working class speech, on the other hand, typical of the industrial areas in central Scotland, provokes general disapproval and is branded as 'slovenly' and 'degenerate'. This latter attitude became institutionalised quite early in the educational system, so that we find, for example, at the turn of the last century, comment from school inspectors about the desirability of excluding 'dialectal' and 'certain Scots peculiarities of speech' from schools.

A statement from 'The Advisory Council's Report on Primary Education in Scotland' in 1946 confirms just how entrenched such institutionalised prejudices were:

> [Scots] is not the language of educated people anywhere and could not be described as a suitable medium of education and culture ... ... because of extraneous influences, it has sadly degenerated and become a worthless jumble of slipshod, ungrammatical and vulgar forms, still further debased by the intrusion of the less desirable Americanisms from Hollywood.

And are: fifty years on, and it would seem that *The Scots Magazine* continues to perpetrate these views. Yet any full account of Scots must include all views. 'Unemployed, Glenboig' is as Scottish as 'Retired, Broughty Ferry'. Scottishness does not mean 'like us': it is as varied as the 5 million odd folk who live here, not to mention Scots abroad. Otherwise the name 'Scots Magazine' begins to sound a little hollow.

The work of writers and artists who are not afraid to incur the wrath of the 'moral majority' – in any society, never mind Scotland in 1996 – is crucial in making sure that social conscience doesn't atrophy. Contemporary Scottish writers have gone a long way towards breaking down the polite conspiracies of silence that, as we know, can conceal serious abuse by supposedly upright citizens, members of the clergy and the social services; political corruption; bold-faced greed given widespread applause as entrepreneurial skill; all the -isms of divisive hatred, and perhaps worst of all, a self-centred complacency acquiesced by those whom Fleming terms the 'haves'. His use of the words 'haves' and 'have-nots' betrays the real bad language here: his own. The possession of cultural rectitude, of 'correct language', underwrites and secures other forms of political control which determine those who are permitted security and purpose in society, and those who are denied it. If such ideological manoeuvres have become familiar through the polemical, passionate subversion of Tom Leonard's 'vulgar eloquence', they are given a new and searing twist in Duncan McLean's *ABC of Bad Language*, where he shows that it is words like poverty and homelessness which are our true 'gutter obscenities'. Fleming's is exactly the attitude which Albert Camus attacks in his essay 'The Artist and his Time', from *The Myth of Sisyphus*:

> ... from my first articles to my latest book I have written so much, and perhaps too much, only because I can't keep from being drawn towards everyday life, towards those, whoever they may be, who are humiliated and debased. They need to hope, and if all keep silent or if they are given a choice between

two kinds of humiliation, they will be forever deprived of hope
and we with them. It seems to me impossible to endure that
idea nor can he who cannot endure it lie down to sleep in his
tower. Not through virtue ... ... but through a sort of organic
intolerance, which you feel or do not feel. Indeed I see many
who fail to feel it, but I cannot envy their sleep.

In recent years, spurred it would seem by just this feeling, Scottish writers have lifted a lot of stones in order to let the light shine in, as Janice Galloway has phrased it. Their efforts deserve better response than malicious envy, or penance on the creepie before the self-appointed elders of the kirk of Scottish culture. For their work in Scotland is not a unilateral assault on delicate sensibility but is in keeping with a broad twentieth century movement which believes that the language of literature cannot deny its 'vulgar' – literally 'of the people' – roots without dying like pretty cut flowers in a vase.

In this movement, the American influence has surely been as important to Scottish writers as elsewhere and this issue of the *Edinburgh Review* features a group whose east-coast emergence in the early 1970s seemed to confirm the new Transatlanticism. Short-lived and wilfully nebulous as 'The Lost Poets' grouping was, it was tempered in the rock and roll furnace of the sixties and was at ease with the idea of performance as one of the writer's roles, organising readings as a means of promoting their work and that of others. As beneficiaries of the establishment of the Scottish Arts Council Literature Department in 1972, Ron Butlin, Brian McCabe, Andrew Greig and Liz Lochhead were members of the first generation to regard being a writer in Scotland as a possible career, instead of having to choose between the high road to England or America as taken by people like Alan Sharp and Gordon Williams in the 1960s, and home-based part-time writing subsidised by other jobs as was common for previous generations.

All four Lost Poets have since gone on to become senior figures in the contemporary scene, moving from poetry into fiction and drama, although the work of the three male writers has at times been overshadowed by the west-coast renaissance led by Gray, Leonard, Kelman and co. While Butlin, McCabe and Greig rightly avoid any suggestion that their work adheres to the dictates of a 'movement' or 'school' – and the impressive versatility and variousness of their respective writings to date will confirm just how misrepresentative such an interpretation would be – we gather the three together again in this issue for two important reasons. Firstly, because their work deserves greater prominence – and in this issue, new writing from Butlin, McCabe and Greig illustrates their continuing influence on contemporary Scottish literature. Secondly, to record the vital role they have performed in pioneering the teaching of creative writing to others – another means of drawing out the voices of the 'inarticulate'. This is an activity which writers, and their students, nowadays take somewhat for granted (assuming a grant is available!), but the labours of the Lost Poets in defining a position for the writer in the community date from before the time when 'Writer-in-Residence' still meant that the door was locked, the 'phone disconnected, and the lonely occupant sweating over a solitary sonnet.

Although the fourth Lost Poet, Liz Lochhead, is not represented in our feature, her place as linkwoman between the Edinburgh-based 'lostology' and the Glaswegian scene of the same period, centred around Phillip Hobsbaum's Glasgow University writers' group, is particularly interesting. In both these circles, active in the early 1970s, the American influence of groups like the Black Mountain Poets and the Beat Generation seems obvious. Indeed, this common link between Scotland west and east at the time is illustrated in this issue by Andrew Greig's memoir of the period, when he recounts meeting Tom Leonard at a reading in Glasgow, where a mention of the name Ed Dorn (once a student at Black Mountain) is sufficient to establish an immediate understanding between them.

This connection is important. Charles Olson, rector of the Black Mountain College from 1951 until 1956, in his manifesto-like *Projective Verse* (1950) laid emphasis on the primacy of spoken language over literary devices of syntax, rhyme and metre. The *Black Mountain Review* (1954-7) edited by one of Olson's students, Robert Creeley, published work by emergent Beats like Ginsberg and Kerouac – and the same Robert Creeley wrote an introduction to an American edition of the works of Robert Burns, in which he quotes Emerson on the national bard: 'the poet of the poor, anxious, cheerful working humanity, so had he the language of low life'. Creeley, whose place in post-war American writing is central, writes that Burns' 'poems and songs were truly among my first delights in hearing and reading poetry as a boy'. It is interesting to consider that an American movement which has so influenced Scottish writing in the last fifty years may have a taproot stretching all the way back to Ayrshire in the early years of American independence – that in discovering the unfettered voice of 1950s America, Scottish writers were reconnecting with their own broken tradition, and so circumnavigating MacDiarmid's high modernism.

The democratization of the language of literature to include the full breadth of Scots and Gaelic voices is by necessity a process of breaking down the many taboos which have haunted linguistic self-confidence, and so freedom of expression, in the past. This is not simply a matter of wilful destruction purely for the sake of it. At the heart of this movement is the desire to represent things as they really are, a feeling that the polite language of literature as it once was has proved incapable of straight-talking. It is a point well made by Tom Leonard in 'On Reclaiming the Local and the Theory of the Magic Thing' from *Edinburgh Review 77*:

> The 'leaders' are separate from their language. Their language is a piece of purchased property held in common amongst themselves. Therefore, when they address you, their being stands at a tangent to what they have expressed; and when one attempts dialogue with that expression one addresses not simply a person but a closed system of value. A closed system of value stands between the two human beings in communication.

When the closed is open and the unspeakable spoken, when the taboos are finally lost, then perhaps we will have a language which meets June Jordan's ideal, where collective identity, including, indeed welcoming, differences of 'power, money, race, gender, age and class', may rightly flourish. Considering the resurgence of Gaelic and Scots, and the push towards a Scottish assembly, there is great relevance for Scotland in Jordan's assertion that:

> ... in a democratic state, our language would have to hurtle, fly, curse and sing, in ... ... all the undeniable and representative and participating voices of everybody here.

In a democratic Scotland, 'the participating voices of everybody here' will surely drown forever the voice of minority government by those who like to see themselves as the 'haves'.

FICTION

DAVID ALMOND

YVONNE D. CLAIRE

R. F. CLERK

IAN HUNT

Buffalo Camel Llama Zebra Ass

David Almond

INSIDE THE ROOF of the blue tent the zodiac was painted in gold. During the interval we stared upward and Colin showed us all which signs we were. The symbols were faded and flaked, were no brighter than the sawdust in the ring far below. The spangles of the trapeze girl as she swung through the lights had been the brightest things up there. Now she walked sadly before us in a tightly-fastened mac and dusty shoes and sold nuts and Mars bars from a tray balanced at her waist.

Margaret knocked me in the ribs.

Colin's a lion, she said. Catherine's a goat. You're an ugly bull.

I know, I said. That's why there's such a stink in here.

But you mustn't believe it, said Colin. It's a pagan thing.

He took out his wallet again and went to the girl and bought chocolate for us all.

They saw animals and gods in the stars, I said. They thought the stars showed what would happen and what they should do.

And we don't believe that, said Mary.

God gave us free will. We choose what to do. We decide whether to be good or to be bad.

We ate the chocolate and waited for the interval to end. I imagined the girl flying across the roof of the tent towards my outstretched arms. Mary asked how she could be twins when there was only one of her. Margaret said she'd like to be the fish, swimming deep down in the sea with seals and dolphins. Catherine said it was best to be the water-carrier, helping thirsty and worn-out travellers, and anyway you just had to stay what you were born as.

The clowns came on and threw buckets of shredded paper at us. They sawed the trapeze girl in two and pretended to forget how to put her together again. She returned with other girls and they stood on the backs of horses that raced furiously around the ring. Men from Russia in singlets and tights balanced from each other's brows on long silver poles. In the posters there'd been elephants and tigers, but neither of them came. The band played in the end, and animals were brought on as a final entertainment for the children. There was a little buffalo, a camel, a llama, a zebra and an ass. They trotted round and round the ring. A Russian stood at the centre, flicking a long whip at them. Such an odd arrangement, so precisely-trained: the muscular wide-horned buffalo; the dusty grunting camel with wobbly hump and gangly legs; the dainty llama with its neck so stiff and its eyes alert; the sprightly synthetic zebra; the poor little damp-eyed ass. From the crowd they drew appreciation, much tender sighing, and of course a little mockery upon themselves.

In the doorway as we filed out from the tent, the trapeze girl in her mac sold models of a monkey who climbed to the top of a ladder and tumbled down again.

Where were the tigers? asked Margaret. Where were the elephants?

The girl turned her sad eyes to us.

They've been poorly, she said. Not well at all.

She shrugged.

Buy them a monkey, she said to Colin, but we turned away and entered the field outside.

It's only a small circus after all, said Colin.

Ass, buffalo, camel, llama, zebra, said Mary. In alphabetical order.

We pondered the truth of this.

So where would the elephant have fitted in? said Catherine.

Too big, said Mary. It'd squash the others.

In the alphabet, nit.

Between camel and llama. And the tiger'd go in after llama and eat them all.

Where would you three go? said Margaret. The goat, the lion and the ugly bull.

We worked it out, told each other. We positioned many more: porcupines, rhinoceros, spiders, moles. We named an animal for each letter, an alphabet of beasts.

Above us the stars began to appear.

Did God give the animals their names? said Mary.

No answer.

When he made them, he must have said what this one was and this one was.

Again no answer.

Are the names we use the same as the names God uses? Does he call the zebra zebra and the camel camel.

We can't know, said Catherine. We just can't know.

We walked on, away from the tent, towards the nearby road

where the bus stops were. Already long queues were forming there.
 Mary put her index fingers out above her brow and played the buffalo. Margaret lowered her head and grunted and hunched her shoulders, a camel. They trotted gently on before us.
 Then came a woman's voice: Who's allowing them to do this?
 We stopped and found Marion McKenna's mother close behind us. Marion was at her side in a tight blue coat, the monkey toy dangling from her hand.
 Do you know that God gave us eternal souls to separate us from all other creatures? said Mrs McKenna.
 Mary and Margaret paused and turned.
 Do you know that?
 We nodded.
 And do you know that it is an insult to God if we lower ourselves and imitate the beast?
 No answer.
 You are in charge of these children, she said. You must not allow them to wander into sin.
 Colin looked down and lit a cigarette.
 Marion stared wide-eyed at us all from behind her mother.
 I could see that Mary and Margaret wanted to laugh.
 You do want to see your Daddy again, don't you? said Mrs McKenna.
 Mary and Margaret returned to us. We faced the woman, the circus lights, the dwindling crowd approaching us and passing by.
 Think about it, she said.
 I thought about it. I thought of everything I'd been told, that his pain was over, that he was in Heaven, that he waited for us there. I thought of him and prayed for him each night, as I'd been told to, even as I felt the faith deserting me.
 Mrs McKenna raised her finger.
 He'll be watching you, she said. Think of your eternal souls.
 And she shook her head, walked on, drew her daughter towards the road.
 Pig, whispered Margaret.
 Cow, whispered Mary.
 We giggled, waited, allowed the woman to get far ahead of us. We searched the sky for the constellations of the zodiac. Colin said that the stars had changed position since the first astrologers had seen the lion, the goat, the bull and all the rest.
 You could make yourself see anything, said Mary. Couldn't you?
 The stars were the spangles of a costume. The trapeze girl was a great arrangement of points of light against the dark.

Will we come back again? said Margaret.

Colin shook his head. No. The circus would travel on.

We moved again across the pale dusty field towards the road.

Can Daddy see us now? said Margaret.

Yes, we all assured her.

We went through the fence, stood in the queue beneath the streetlights. Behind us, the summit of the blue tent mingled with the sky.

What would happen if we called the zebra camel? said Mary.

We laughed and gave the animals the names of other animals.

What's a horse? said Mary.

A dog, said Catherine.

No, a goose.

Stop it, Michelle, I said to Mary.

Sorry, Simon, she answered.

A bus came, and the first half of the queue climbed aboard. Mrs McKenna watched us sternly through the window. Marion played gently with the monkey.

Margaret turned her face up to the light and closed her eyes. Catherine put an arm around her.

Yes, he can, she whispered. Yes. Yes.

Soon the next bus came, we climbed aboard.

Catherine Colin Margaret Mary Me.

David Almond was born in Felling on Tyne and lives in Newcastle. His first collection *Sleepless Nights* was published by Iron Press. He edited the fiction magazine *Panurge* from 1987 till 1993.

WINNING ENTRY (PREVIOUSLY PUBLISHED AUTHOR CATEGORY) IN THE EDINBURGH REVIEW SHORT STORY COMPETITION 1995.

Over, all Over and Beyond

Yvonne D. Claire

'ECOUTE,' I said, 'listen, don't do that.' I kicked him, not too hard, and moved away towards the other end of the bar. Next thing I knew he'd scrambled to his feet from where he'd been groping about on the floor, looking up my skirt, and was following me, slowly, his face closed-up and dark, a hunter's face, his right hand clenched into a fist. I almost tripped over the legs of one of the stools and steadied myself against the rail that ran along the counter: 'Felix, please, he's going to –' Felix didn't even lift his head, just squinted at the glass he'd been polishing, twirling it in his fingers. The man was almost up against me now. I tried to back away, but I'd reached the wall. 'Tu vois ça? Yes?' his fist coming closer; inch by inch he was raising his fist towards me, with the deadly concentration of a drunk. A smell, acrid and overpowering, monkey hairs on knuckles. I wanted to throw up my arms and push him away, I wanted to scream, toss my head. Instead, something pierced the small of my neck –

I was sitting on the floor, propped up against the bar, and Felix was pouring cold water over me. My neck hurt, and I felt a little dazed. 'Better?' Felix asked, dangling the empty pitcher. I managed a small grin, 'Hmm, thanks. You got a spare towel by any chance?

Someone touched my shoulder: 'Vois donc, please you see ...' The voice stung me to the quick. What was *he* still doing here? Had nobody called the police?

I struggled to get up, when suddenly a fist swung in front of my eyes. Fingers began to unclasp one by one and there, cutting grimy rings into the flesh, lay several coins on an open palm. 'You see,' the hand shook slightly, 'always it has money under bar. I find. For beer, tu vois?' He laughed, loud and happily, while behind him on the wall a huge sea urchin swayed to and fro, to and fro, for no reason at all. I could have cried like a child.

Meanwhile Ramon would be jabbering away at one of his interminable conferences that I'd given up accompanying him to. South Africa this time: far, so far. He was never around when I needed him. That was the first lesson I'd learnt in the four months of our marriage.

I went and stood on the terrace. The sea breeze had died down, and the air pressed round me thick and silent, cloying as candy floss. Two dogs were chasing each other along the curve of the lagoon, dodging the tourists draped on leafy hotel towels like offerings. Every so often the smaller, fawn-coloured one would roll over and lie completely still, its throat turned towards the glint of the other's teeth.

A shame their fight wasn't for real. The island was rampant with those skinny mongrels. Worse than the cockroaches they were. Howling and scavenging and copulating all over the place. Giving birth in the cemetery. Giving birth non-stop, it seemed, until their teats were ragged and trailing in the dirt. Later you'd come across them by the roadside, even the male dogs bloated now and breeding ... whatever. Blowflies. New life.

Ramon always said I wouldn't have any problems finding a job as an English teacher down here, 'Of course not, with your qualifications, your experience.' Sometimes he made it sound more like a question; he wasn't a native speaker, after all. I still had my girl-guide enthusiasm then and wanted to believe such reassurances, whispers so silky soft and phosphorescent they spin a cocoon around you until, snap! you wake up, all alone, and it's night, and there's a storm going on, drowning the prowl of footsteps outside. The muddy footprints are washed away again by the rain. Apart from one – which you discover next morning, just beside the back door, when you check the bungalow and garden for storm damage.

A gust of wind had risen from the spiky green stillness of the sugar-cane fields beyond the village, lifting my T-shirt, still wet from Felix's pitcher, and slapping it against my belly, hard, almost viciously. The flame-breasted bird that had been sipping drops of water from an aircon pipe flew up in a fright. The land breeze had started, it would be dark soon. I picked up my bag and went down the steps, down and away to where the beach was empty, walking quite slowly to feel the sand sifting through my toes.

I avoided the hotels and gave Coom at the boat-house, gap-toothed Coom with his skin the colour of scorched wood and as brittle, a wave instead. Only today I was being stupid, thoughtless really, because he waved back and there was something in his hand. I shielded my eyes from the glare. A flipper. He was brandishing a flipper, he was hitting out at the distance between us, smacking it, and shouting words in Creole. My heart tightened and my hand fell stiffly to my side as I carried on, a little faster now. What was he doing that for? Another game of hide and seek à la mauricienne? The longer you lived on this island, the less you understood, and the less you ... I held my breath, quite stunned: Or did Coom *know* about the footprint outside the bungalow? Did he ...? Had he ...? – Inside me was a heap of scree someone had trodden on.

At first I thought I was going to be sick and dropped on all fours, panting. But nothing happened, except that for a while I couldn't see anything; it was like snow blindness in a country without snow. Once the grains of sand and tiny shells had trickled back where they belonged I got up. The tide was out and the rocks lay hunched in the shallows, fuzzy shapes, barely under the surface. If you went too close, the coral that bristled all over their shoulders, nasty brown coral like the matted hair of a giant, would etch blood lines on your skin. The water had lost its pre-storm clearness; it had a murky, troubled look, as if thousands of sea cucumbers were steaming away furiously.

Nowhere was safe ground anymore. How could I make Ramon understand? He who'd studied law and firmly believed you couldn't lose your footing as long as you kept within certain boundaries, boundaries staked out by the society you were part of. Which society was I part of anyway? In the mud just in front of me were my own marks, nicely symmetrical, from toes, knees and spread hands, two adjoining squares, like cages.

Even the 'Dundee Lion' had stopped being neutral territory, with its drunks creeping and crawling around the bar stools in the half-light, scaring off the other customers. When all I'd hoped for was to meet some expats, feel their sympathy. Felix was British, of course, but I didn't really want to tell *him*; he wasn't the type to share confidences with somehow.

I turned to go, then suddenly found myself facing the sea again, crouching now, and my fingers were grubbing and clawing into the sand, hurling it away by the fistful, angry, spluttering arches of dirt right over the six marks I'd made, over, all over and beyond. Finally I set off towards the road and the bungalow's cunning system of padlocks.

Ever since school through to university and teacher training college I'd gone for men whose names started with 'M'. So why I've ended up with Ramon I'm not sure. Unless it's because he's Mauritian and his surname's Mitchell. Occasionally, just as a joke, I make up acronyms: when I'm in a cold and windy mood I call him Moran, for its Scottish ring; when I feel hot and barbarous, he becomes Maron, which I pronounce with double 'r' like the French for 'chestnut' – after all, his skin's as brown and shinily smooth. Ramon doesn't mind, at least not in private. In public, of course, he is lawyer Ramon Mitchell, with a degree from Oxford and a bank account in Switzerland, smug and slightly arrogant.

We'd met on the Edinburgh-Glasgow train one early Friday evening about a year ago. He'd just got himself a cup of coffee from the trolley, and the vendor wouldn't accept his twenty, 'New regulations, I'm afraid; all those forgeries ...' I sat watching them act it all out in the darkness of the window, feeling as high as a kite after a few end-of-the-week drinks with some colleagues. Well, I had plenty of loose change on me, so what the hell – I gestured to the woman, then smiled at him across two empty rows of seats.

The sun was almost touching the horizon by now, its rays slanting pale and yellow through the feathery leaves of the filao trees by the beach. It sank much more rapidly out here than at home, or what I used to call home – because I was at home here now, wasn't I? – so rapidly that nightfall still caught me by surprise sometimes, like a door being shut in my face. I walked faster, I must get back to the bungalow before dark. My bag was knocking against my hip with every step, and inside the bag was the jingling. Always the jingling. I imagined the keys, the metal blistery and greasy from the heat, sliding about on the ring, twisting, their bits touching, then gripping and hooking into each other, barely long enough, before clattering apart to start all over again. Damn those keys, the whole frigging bunch of them.

I clamped the bag under my arm and hurried on. To my left, a cock began to screech behind the corrugated-iron fencing round a shack and banana tree, and I nearly stumbled over the hen that had come rushing through a gap squawking and flailing its wings.

Before we bought our rings I said to Ramon: 'But I'll never be a submissive wife, even living in the Indian Ocean won't change that. You'd better warn your mother straightaway.'

He stared at me for a moment, his eyes black and glittering as a gecko's, then he began to laugh. Soon he was rocking and roaring with laughter. He laughed so much his face puckered up into a crisscross of lines, and I had to slap him on the back: 'Ha-ha-harder,' he gasped, 'come on, harder ...' What on earth was the matter with him? I hadn't meant to be funny. And my hand was getting sore too, as if his spine was making gashes into it. All of a sudden he fell quiet, pulled me close. 'Don't worry,' he said, stroking my cheeks and down to what he calls the bird's belly under my chin, 'she'll be expecting that. And there won't be any reading of sheets after *our* wedding night ...' The palm of my hand was marbled red and white; I tried not to swallow, waiting for the pain to ease off.

Across the street, the road workers I'd passed earlier were leaning against the wall of a shop that doubled as a bar, drinking.

'Ça va?' they called out in their strange singsong.

I hesitated, 'Oui, ça va bien.' I never quite knew how to behave in a situation like this; whether to simply ignore the people or nod, smile even; whether to greet them.

'Hé, hé!' One of the workers was gesturing with his bottle of Phoenix. When he saw me looking, he took a swig, licked the froth off his lips and cried, 'Ah! Ah! AAAH!'

The others started laughing.

I could have spat at them. Had they, too, heard I was alone out there, at the bungalow? Who had told them, though? My face was wetter than ever, streaming with sweat. Why was everybody trying to frighten me? It wasn't my fault I still hadn't found a job, still wasn't earning any money. Why were they all cutting the ground from under my feet, hacking it up into clods, then half-clods, finally crumbs and grit? Quicksands. Already the colours were fading into shadows; a few more minutes and it would be night, pitch-black night.

It wasn't much further now. But what then? What was I to do? Perhaps if I managed to get hold of Ramon he'd try to re-route his flight and return a day or two early; if I explained about the footprint, surely he'd understand. Because he'd rung only yesterday, before the storm, to ask how I was. 'So-so,' I'd said in my brightest voice, guilty at making him feel guilty and yet wanting him to feel the weight.

The deserted bungalow – Every gate along the street reminded me, every door. And behind the gates, the doors –

Well, nothing. Don't be silly. Nothing except the cockroaches holed up in their crevices or scuttling in cupboards and behind the cooker; and the geckos, of course, all turquoise and emerald and jade, amiably slinking up to an insect, then spurting yet another mural. Remember how you secured and snibbed, how you bolted, locked and fastened yourself out of that bungalow, all the way from the rooftop down to the spiderwebbed larder window in the basement? You checked and double-checked. That in itself was pretty ridiculous, let's be honest. For it was *outside* you'd found the footprint. One single footprint outside a door you'd kept religiously locked. Could be you'd forgotten about the gate and left it open, and some tramp wandered in to shelter from the foul weather. So you went and matched up traces of mud on the verandah until you had convinced yourself, worked yourself up into a state.

But I used not to be like that. I used not to be afraid of things before. Not even of the dark in the city with its shadows falling across doorways, blanketing empty spaces. And certainly not of a dark like this, a dark full of sunheat and laughter and the sounds of the ocean against the reef ...

A group of people have emerged from the well-lit apartment block ahead; for an instant the wind's afloat with scraps of conversation, shouts, the slam of car doors, an engine starting up. Seconds later their headlights are in my eyes and the night shatters, then reforms. A few houses away the giant banyan tree, its roots and branches all tangled-up and entwined, is a looming blackness. After the tree I'll have to take the dirt road –

Maybe I shouldn't go back to the bungalow and just ring Ramon from here; there's a payphone over at Ali's grocery store. But I don't have his number. It's on a slip of paper somewhere in that twilight kitchen slashed by shadows ... Who else –? How about Kistna for a change? Kistna, my good old mother-in-law, and yet almost a stranger. She'll be so glad to hear from me. She'll ask lots of questions and talk freely. And if I tell her of the footprint she'll do her best to help.

I'm about to cross when a dog breaks into a howling bark nearby. Its fierceness snaps at me, rips right into me. Yes, Kistna will do her very best. She'll be only too anxious to help. In tones as slithery as her saris she'll dish out her warnings, speak of wifely duties, of strength and endurance. Lovingly she'll feed my fears, pat them into place. Damn her.

But that leaves only the beach. No, more than that: the strays, the sea. Me and the sea and the strays and the beach. Perhaps the moon. Yes, the moon, too. All the stars even. That's quite enough.

And such a sight it will be: the ocean whip-lashed into froth rearing up snorting and kicking against the barrier and tearing off bits of coral bones spitting them across into the lagoon, and the lagoon itself in a bile-coloured frenzy with coconuts tossing and clashing on the waves like dead men's heads.

Yvonne D. Claire is Swiss and now lives in Edinburgh with her husband and their dog.

WINNING ENTRY (NEWLY PUBLISHED AUTHOR CATEGORY) IN THE EDINBURGH REVIEW SHORT STORY COMPETITION 1995.

Head

R. F. Clerk

IT WAS THE YELLOW HALL this time. Here the cell windows didn't open and had bars on the outside. As he was being escorted through the gates into the Hall he noticed, through an open door, that his old block now had a goldfish tank near the telly. He was put in a cell on the ground floor of yellow Hall with another prisoner who was in his forties. The cell had two double bunks although there were only the two of them in there.

While he was in this cell he went with the others to sew mailbags. They all took needle and thread, the thirty or forty of them, and sat down in rows to mend the bags. He tired of this and rose from his front row seat and went over to the sinks where he picked up a bar of white soap with the imperial stamp on it. At least he was under her protection – he was one of her agents. With the soap he began writing on the wall, drawing a graph and the circled letter A for anarchy. The prison officers sat by the door quietly observing him, then he sat down again. The crafts instructor, in a brown coat, took up a hose and began washing down the dust on the floor. It *was* dusty – the prisoners might die of some lung disease he felt; he got up and told another prisoner that he was a customs officer, ordering him to pass over the hammer on the table – he refused. Picking up the hammer himself he went over and smashed a window. The prison officers rushed up, and grabbed him, manhandling him out of the workshop back to his cell.

He was taken to see the governor in his office. There was a pair of pictures hanging on the wall, one at either end of the room, in monochrome, of the Queen and the Duke of Edinburgh. He stood between the two officers and answered the governor that he did it to let fresh air into the workshop – it was dusty there. He lost several days remission, but he remained in the same cell.

Now and again he was taken along with the others to the showers and once he had exercise with several hundred prisoners walking round and round in a huge yard. The clouds were low and gloomy – guards stood in long, black overcoats and caps, watching. One of the officers, that one, the tall one, he thought, was the Duke of Gloucester. The mass of brown serge continued to circle, in threes and fours, talking among themselves – a low mumbling, and shuffling of ill-fitting shoes breaking over the vast yard like the beaching waves of a desolate sea.

He was by himself until he saw another fellow on his own who looked rather weak and, feeling the stronger, he walked up to him and asked how he was, and what he was in for. He was a young fellow with dark hair and brown eyes who grinned and said, 'Arson.' He frowned as he knew that was a serious offence, but walked round once with him and then sat down amongst the others. A lad asked him where he was from – his head felt like a lump of concrete, but he replied, 'Aiberdeen.' The lad grinned and said, 'Ken the Blue Lampie?'

He knew it – a pub in the city up the Gallowgate which he hardly ever went in, but he was not inclined to talk and needed a pee. He got up on his feet, and asked an officer where the toilets were. He indicated a long, concrete bunker which he went over to. It was indeed the toilet and, from its bunker-like structure, he deduced that this was where the guards hid when the German planes came over and slaughtered the prisoners at exercise. He only had exercise in this yard a couple of times before things took a turn for the worse.

One night he lay on his bunk in his cell looking at the wall. He noticed a shadow pattern on it where the sodium lamps outside shone through the bars of the unblinded window. Earlier he had broadcast stories to the nation from *Sielanka* – a book of Polish stories he found in the Hall bookcase. It was a radio transmission from his cell. This was a serious time for the country as he had heard of the pub bombings in Birmingham and the marches by the National Front. He declared a national alert – he was the Helmsman – and, as he saw a shadow form a cross on the wall, he knew he was one of the Warriors of Christ the King. If only they could hold on, everything would be alright. He had a strenuous task tracking the I.C.B.M.s across the wall, but he did it – they all went over to America. Now, though, he was concerned about his family, as he had turned over and seen that the ventilator was stuffed up with papers. The rest of his family who were, he thought, in the prison would suffocate – he hauled the papers out. The other prisoner, hearing him, turned over and, irritated by his continual talking, told him to put them back. He refused and, jumping up, pressed the buzzer. A guard came, and asked him what the trouble was, and then three of them carted him off to solitary in his underpants which they stripped him of and threw in a mattress and blanket. The door boomed shut.

He got out of there after a while, and was back in the yellow block, this time with a ginger-haired, worried-looking fellow. A black officer stood outside the cell door – from Robben Island he surmised. A couple of copies of an anarchist newspaper were thrown in – 'Here's yer book,' an officer sneered – and he was left to himself, the ginger-haired fellow having departed. He thought he was from the Workers Revolutionary Party as a preponderance of them seemed to have ginger hair. However, he was not satisfied with his paper – he could not concentrate to read and the print hurt his eyes. He turned to the window and looked out into the exercise yard to see a wagtail hopping along the ground, but he was not going to be the Birdman of Alcatraz and, in a sudden fit of anger, upended his bed and smashed the window. Two guards dragged him out and a third, a nasty looking, young fellow with greying hair, came up. He had fallen to the floor and thought the officer was going to kick his head in. He didn't but they navigated him to another cell at the end of the Hall and flung him in.

He spent most of his sentence in this cell which was opposite the control room for close observation. Once, when the door was left open, he walked out and up the iron stairs to the first floor but the officer in charge boomed out 'Logan!' and he came down. The cell was bare except for the chanty, and the mattress and blankets he had at night. Scored on the wall were black bootmarks like the flames of a fire and from somewhere he heard the phrase 'Face the fire'. He heard other things such as 'Trotsky-fascist' and 'High-flier' – phrases which he had never heard before. At one point he became so immersed in East European politics that he thought they were going to execute him for his involvement. He had a joke which frightened him, which was, what would happen if he got the chop? He got a steak pie – he was reprieved. He always enjoyed his meals, though now they were brought to him in his cell, whereas previously he had gone to the dining hall, where he broke and chewed chicken bones between his teeth to extract the marrow; it was a ploy to signal his desperation. What also frightened him was the proverbial possibility of becoming a vegetable – he could remember the word 'canteen' which was used for the sweets, jam, and toothpaste the prisoners could buy in the Hall every week, but he could not recall the word for the place where he used to have meals with the other prisoners. He knew it was not 'canteen' or 'restaurant'; the word escaped him and worried him. Exercise he had only every other day. He was locked up alone in his cell, but every morning they took him for a wash and sometimes he had a shave and a shower.

Wretched though he might be, he knew he would not be there for ever, unlike the prison officers who were there for life. He felt sorry for some – they looked ill and enervated. They had grey hair, puffy white faces, sunken eyes and had the air of being resigned to their fate. Sometimes, even, they cared for him – they took away the razor when he went on too long with it while shaving, or confiscated his glass jar of jam which he had bought and kept in his cell. But there was one, a shortish, plump man with ginger hair who worried him. He came in with a brown sheet which said something about his expected release and asked him to sign it. He could not read it and refused to sign which made the guard angry.

Then one morning the fellow opened the cell door suddenly which made him jump up with fright as he thought he was going to kick him in the back as he lay in his blanket. He took the first opportunity to defend himself, by attack; he punched 'Droopy' as he called him on the shoulder out in the Hall and immediately three or four guards pounced on him, pounding and kicking him. A particularly heavily built guard then hauled him into his cell, propped him up against the corner, and slammed his fist into his stomach – he collapsed in a heap onto the hot water pipe like in the Westerns.

He was alone in his cell and played games to himself; in the corner sticking out from under the linoleum was a piece of white plastic with three or four black 'peaks' on it as in a mountain range of which one peak was Churchill, another Atatürk. His horsehair mattress was bound together by pieces of string and little strips of cloth in red, white, and electric blue – the colours of Poland he believed, which he saved by stuffing them through the ventilator. He fought to save Poland and so called his cell 'Poland' as it had a 'Po' in the corner. The electric blue stood for the buffer states of Eastern Europe, from Finland to Hungary and Yugoslavia, the significance of the electric blue in the mattress substantiated by the arrival of *The Magic Mountain* by Thomas Mann in the bookcase outside his cell – a 'book-bomb' in cream and electric blue cover. Another book-bomb was *The Malakov Affair* which reminded him of Molotov cocktails. But the most significant was the arrival of the *New English Bible* which had a gold cross on the spine, the anarchist cross of Nechayev. He tried to read it at first, then tore it up and used it for lavatory paper.

The hot water pipe was blue, and set across the cell below the window with a z-bend at one corner. He lay with her and serenaded her; it was the railway line from Waverley to Glasgow Queen Street and from Central to Stranraer along which the Northern Irish bombers commuted; it was part of the engines in the bowels of the flagship of the Royal Navy in which he was an artificer; it was part of a submarine which went 'Zube, Zube, Zube' in the night, or

'Puck, Puck Puck' as the captain of the flagship hunted the sub down. One of his distant relations was an admiral of the fleet, at least he had the same family name, and for the Polish Army, he had a Polish uncle. The prisoners *were* the Polish Army in their brown serge uniforms. He draped his towel over the pipe and broadcast, via the multi-coloured, chequered inlay in the middle of the towel, his dispatches which the constables at the police station picked up on their chequered hats.

But at times his games overtook him: when he thought Mussolini was in the cell above; when he gave Hirohito the fascist salute as the emperor sent his airmen to their deaths; when he remembered Ralph Ellison of *Invisible Man* and Jim Morrison of *The Doors* – for these two he saw black light and a constellation of falling, pink stars. Then he looked at the flagpole over the gate of the prison – it had turned into a radio mast, no flag was to be seen and they were using him as a human radio to transmit through. Utter horror.

At other times, in the middle of the night, he would hear the human masses of an estate nearby roaring outside as a terrorist, arms cache had been found; he would get up and bellow at them to shut up. Sometimes the prison nurses – he knew they were so – came in with measures of Largactil or an injection, but one day he held up his hand like the Red Hand of Ulster and they never came back after that. But it all came to an end.

The guard who had punched him in the stomach, the Hungarian, came into his cell one night and said he was getting out the next day. He was pleased but only after he had ripped his card off his cell door and flung it in the bin, to leave the black, metal, card holder flying the flag of anarchy. Some of the prisoners had spoken to him by his name and asked him what he was going to do when he got out; he replied that he would study at Cambridge.

In the morning, around seven or eight, his cell door was opened and he was told he was being released. He had to slop out his cell, but he had no breakfast before being taken round to reception where he donned his green corduroy jacket, green trousers and his new, black boots. And then he was free to go.

But they had not broken his spirit – he had hidden his soul in his tooth, his canine tooth, the part of his body that would last the longest.

R. F. Clerk formerly wrote under the pen name Paul Logan

The Daubers

Ian Hunt

> Bombardment with verbal ballast does not mean that the word has lost its significance. It is like a disease which *arrives on foot and leaves on horseback*.
> – Jiří Kolář

IF NOT THIS, that, if not that, this, pah, a swizz. Always choices, a little bit heretical, but chosen and arranged and deranged and in different orders. I say chosen, you will know what I mean by that, as by choices, I mean I was dealt them. And they stuck to me, or I to them, and we became somehow familial, all too long ago now. So this and that, and this against that, and this mistaken for that. Your word against mine is all we have to show. And so I swapped you for it, hah, done. Standing where you stand, just the same. And no better. As in children's games, it scarcely matters who dealt the blow or received it. Enter a magician. To a children's party, he never got to do the grownups. The original swindle of being forced to attend. And behind this, the smaller grouping, not a party, nothing to celebrate or name special, their days. A place for the small one, a place for the middle one, and a place for the biggest. And one which was just right. Someone having left. Most probably a person already having left. Call that a certainty. And walls of wood, wood all around, outside trees in their mixture of dying and budding parts, spotted with scale, inside everything of wood if possible to make it from wood. And the same old porridge was served up all over again, it came back day after day, they didn't know where from, they put the bowls out clean in the morning, went out to do their work, which was a kind of play, and in the evening there would be porridge. Enter a magician, addled after beatings on the journey, marked on the left brow. He knocked, waited. Knocked again, gathered himself up, invited himself in, sat down, knocked on the rude table. Brigands, he said, reaching up to cover one half of his face. They did not know what he meant by that, they were standing together to watch him. He knocked on the table and waited. And turned the bowls upside down, and moved them from place to place, the one from the end going in the middle of the other two, the one from the other end going in the new middle between the old middle and the other end. You know the rest. And yet the one that had been in the middle had something still of the middle about it. So a leapfrog from one end to the other, for the sake of artistic variation. He righted the bowls and produced, so, nothing, so, again nothing, so, a dog-rose. A pretty flower, a very pretty one. And tucked it in his lapel and waited. He announces that he is their provider, their mystery. They did not know, were not accustomed to know, whether he was, or how to be sure, or how to doubt, or what a provider is, they have all they want. They were still puzzled why he had moved the bowls so, never having seen a trick before. They did not know when to laugh or clap, and were inclined to say yes, he was the provider, meaning the provider of the flower, the dog-rose, which they knew grew thereabouts. The provisions of porridge being, apparently, a quite separate matter. They had, dimly, some notions of forbears.

And he didn't leave, neither was he invited to stay, he was asleep in the vegetable patch in the morning, they prodded him not sure if he was dead or alive, for they knew that distinction, as the confused states inbetween of insects, for example, which lie very still, move only their horns, sometimes not those, do not appear to eat, die, be born, arrive, leave, simply find a crumpled bag or leaf to lie in, somewhere dark and suitable. You move them out of the house in the morning and find another in the evening, at the exact spot. You bash them with a stone and still they twitch, the broken pieces move. Likewise, in a roundabout way, with sleeping magicians, mouth agape, damp with dew. They prodded him and he started, moved further away, but didn't go entirely. Sleeping after sunrise. There was no one to appeal to, no obvious wrong done, no wrath shown, the man clearly wanted something but he was incapable of explaining it, they had no way of knowing why he'd come or if he'd go eventually. The porridge arrived as usual, or in double portions, or tainted, or hastily prepared, or not at all, if, that is, it wasn't after all cabbage. Which cannot be determined, divine prohibition, all curtained in mystery, god-vaunted uncertainty, apply in writing.

That must be several days and nights. There. A little story about everyone having a bowl, and the mornings and the evenings, and the play and the blessings, and that all changing with the man-magician and his stories and his promises, and everyone confused as to whether the life they had just was, or if it was dedicated to something else. But a story. There might be more, or others, it depends on what's called for, what's taken for what, on the call for explanations, and what the explanations bring in tow. On blitheness disturbed. How you can stare at a bundle of sticks, for example, we proceed by examples, it hangs at the doorpost, and you walk under it time and time again, on the way in and on the way out, morning and evening, until it's pointed out to you that the bundle might fall, or the bindings rot, with certain results, calamitous, you weep at the thought of it, idiot tears, for the people who would weep, for the supposed broken brow, your own. So you wind down the bundle, it is on a pulley and grey rope, inspect the bundle, top and bottom, attempt to break the bundle, standing on one leg, the bundle across the knee, but it holds, it is in a fine state, you set it down and hoist it up again. That is a good bit, when the pulley works though exposed to dust and the sun's heat and the rain, and the rope is again signed off in its figure-of-eight. And you think, so I am aware of the systems governing entry here, but who instigated them, that I don't know. You wonder is it a motto, a sign, a tradesman's sign, we are back to the goldfinch on its gilt chain.

And then it all floods back, dimly, a motto, together we are weak, alone we are strong, was that it? A motto of some kind is required, at a doorpost, wedged in, enjambed. And then if it is a tradesman's sign, you wonder will people ask you for things and if so what price you will set on them, tourists might come. The things were not for sale, but they can be bought, if asked for, you have been asked, or imagine the possibility, and must reply, not wishing to look foolish or lost for words.

– Is this a shop or not?

– It's not a shop, they're for looking at and picking up and putting down again.

– What do you mean they're just for looking at?

– I don't know what I mean, sir, I mean what I say. I like to call a stick a stick. The owner is absent, I am a mere bystander, minding my business.

– You call that business?

– I don't call it anything other than what it is, sir, and now, for the third time, I deny any knowledge of what His Absent Majesty the keeper meant by it, and wish you good morning. And I looked at my pretty, my bird, and she turned away without so much as a chirp.

Faithless insubordinate. None of which is half enough, running away like that, where to run away to after all? And instead of the bundle, now the goldfinch to explain, no better. The family crest, on its gilt chain, with its tinkling song, a companion for a life of trade. We are stuck with it, though I am too tired now to go through that old rigmarole, the nightly treks along the tram lines, not wishing to come home, the borrowed flat, the adoption. An obvious feint, sit him out, he'll manage, the whole pack of him. And so he does, indentured labour, you think he won't? To spite you and himself, fearing a glut. He has his own reasons. And so stuffed, having introduced the subject, we note the connexion of goldfinch and bundle, family likeness, winched up as a sign, to say someone's in. Perhaps it is himself that is in, perhaps he is coming in now, after the night trek, the tentative knocking. Doubtful, on the face of it. But instead of the bundle, the goldfinch, instead of the rope, the golden chain, instead of the doorpost, the courtyard, lemonade, civilization, floodlamps. And where was dark and forested, is now light, without a concomitant moment of dawn when all is allowed to possess its own colour, its own light, we are in the bright courtyard and the door is closed now. Some new ruse. They've got their lights trained on me, but I can still be mindful of that hour. The light is always borrowed but there is an hour when we say it is owned, it pleases us to say that, that it inheres, we cannot bear that it is dark inside, *which in my bosom's shop is hanging still*, in the face of which new brightness, *before us all was whitewash and distemper*, I will be mindful of the colours, *dark in the arse*. Lemon yellow, dried blood, chalk white, lamp black, set off against an ivory ground. The light was Dutch it is said, a Dutch light, it was described to me, making the dawn last all day by spreading gray silt was it, making the creaturely things part of a whole, impossible, I don't believe a word of it, they must be chained down and bolted in place, they're getting to me. It is bright by fluorescence, it is black night yet bright, a humming light source strapped to the wobbling head, confused with an eye, a big eye. Locked in visibility. There are no dark places for the things to go to, no dark places for them to hide themselves, they want to hide, it is sociable, it is natural do so when ashamed, to wish to keep something in reserve, to not be entirely convertible, to be reserved when alone, the old promptings, I'll follow them. The light has no mercy, I blame the attendant, the pupil, Fabritius, who said *white is the new black*, or some such thing. Which is a skill, a sellable skill, the use of words so, but I'll pass them by, they're no good to me, and did him no good, I mean by them only the alternation of light for dark, dark for light, and the creaturely hour which I do mourn, which is excised and quickly gone. I remember it but faintly. There has been nothing but dark and light, you shut your eyes, same result, one or the other. Who to believe? The sadness of the variety we now confront, it is time for idiot tears again, and they do come. The sadness lying in the alternation without the transformation scene, the alarm bell reaction-speeds required. And the indecent opulence, the despair is full of bits and pieces. It's an exaggeration, the sadness, despair, the attendant tears, perhaps blankness is what I mean, smiling like a toy, I shall break it, the goldfinch refused my eye but I didn't think to blame it, we had had one another too long, I put it down to modesty, or vanity, or conceit, but I never blamed her.

There mordant and pretty, my goldfinch again, after-dinner speech material, a friend for life, as my pipe, an Algerian briar. It probably meant something, the bird, but to me it was a bird first, both mordant and pretty. There was a motto too but these things have their moment, in a sudden will to the way of the world, they dwindle, it's impolite to insist you know the truth of them when they are clearly in such a parlous state, patched, shiny with grease. *My Goldfinch Had No Motto. A Talent For Swindling Donneau's Chair. A Fondness For Vertebrates. Effects Of The War On Sheep, With A Note on Goats. My Mordant. Captive Love. Pearl Who We Called Dolly. The Daubers. The Reign of Shoddy. History of Rain, and Other Forms of Precipitation. Our Lives Were Swiss. Excessively Sanguine in A Flood. In The Long Run. To Be Docile.* I have to set them all to work, all of my mottoes, my memoirs, be about your business, my mottoes for all occasions. There, a flood of them, a positive deluge, off or on at will, gushing everywhere, the glut of confession is somewhat to be feared, in my books. But I needs must recollect myself a little. They dazzled me with their wretched lights. I was *trained* for this kind of work, I have the qualifications to prove it. I can always pick myself up again. At the age of seven I started out as a baker's hand. I picked fruit, trod cabbage for pickling, fetched balls at tennis courts, learned carpentry, wrote detective stories and stories about cowboys and indians, was unemployed, worked as a hod-carrier at construction sites, I was an editor, servant, loiterer, sewage-labourer, errand-boy, deliveryman, I worked in the fields and in the forests, as a carpenter, as a navvy, concrete-mixer, pulled carts, I was a watchman, waiter, writer, nursing aide, youth worker, lens-grinder, textbook-writer, lithographer, vendor, public speaker, I helped out in a butcher's and barber's shop, I was the editor-in-chief of a weekly and in a publishing house and I wrote poetry. I've got all the qualifications, but they don't accept them in this country. Insufficiently indented they said. Try telling that to my masters I said. My masters did right by me and I did right by my masters, you got a proper training in all kinds of workmanship, not like here, stuff you, your poxy trade magazine, your flagship branch, the whole pack of you. *Mugging At Matins. Hunger, Said The Plaintiff. Three Had One Over. Offset Upsets. General Theory Of Magic. Universal Funeral Speeches. The*

First Bank Holidays. Life On A Shelf. Défense d'Entrelarder. De Luxe Interment. Cash Flow Our Way. Badigeonnage. The Winning Charade. An odd kind of a shop it was got me the training, he'll weep for the sugar paper twists next. But there's no call for it any more, that kind of work, people do ask but I've forgotten who the suppliers are and to be frank it's not worth our while, until you come here asking for it, are you a personal friend of the patent-holder? Ah well, there is always my bird, I forget which side of the counter I'm on but the bird still won't look at me, she's conceited that way, she loves me, I tell myself she does. I've had about twenty of them now, but I call her my bird, they don't live long, but she reminds me of the first, of Mordant.

From here on it's rash, it's a guess, a loose plank, transfer weight ahead carefully, it's important, you'll fall eitherway, probably backwards. So I say because, it's rash, you have to, in this to and fro of small things jumping up and deranging, so light are they, landing us back where we started, the goldfinch or its placard, if a placard, exposing the fixing on nail and wire, banged into plaster, I cannot abide things to float. We won't ask who's in today, start knocking at the board, strain, all these visitations from magicians or the people who say they are, the fake vagrants, the lookers not takers, I'm not interested in them, only in the fidgets, I want to hold on to them. The children must have fidgeted, or looked at one another, something must have shown in the faces, not closed off, not yet accepting, they did not know what to do, the eldest felt it worst, most probably, the lack of instructions. Also the middle one. As here now, someone clearly had a good plan from which the most basic questions like yours, mine, have been expunged, childish questions but to the point. There is no information, hearsay only, as to whether these simple objects left are mine or someone else's. What legal light that throws on the sin or not of destroying them, after what period de facto ownership might be established, when secure against irredentist claims, whether bequeathed by primo- or ultimogeniture, can only be guessed. Or gainsaid. You see there is no term for the middle one, he is left out. But we are even-handed here. We shall give him a name. I shall name him Donneau, or Dan, because I like his face. There's an economic principle at work. The others don't need their names, but he does, so we've given him one, it's his. Fiat. Though I don't know what the contest is about. I can only say with certainty that there was a wand, a withie, a baton, a switch, this is all shaded in verbiage, and with it though not in writing, a phrase. I can't explain it better than that: *an action involving wood.*

Which must have been the substance of their play, as I understand it, at the corners of the story, the days of work known as play: whittling, hollowing, chewing the pulp, binding, splinting the table leg, making a roof. Or more than one roof, was it each one made, I can't dare the plural, it's too unpredictable. Two or three of them, or both is it, I can't tell. So to go under roofed places apart from the cottage, places of their own making, places not known, and the ruck about the bowls and the relative size of portions, that was clearly not the important matter. And so the story betrays a fatal lack of the unities about the midriff, and you can't be sure if they knew what the water was coming out of his eyes, it might have been merely dew, or the effect of the onions, or something for the insects to drink. He appeared to have some knowledge of beetles, and would stare at them for hours. But the props, the notched sticks to rest laterals, they are all missing, particularly the work that was a kind of play and whether the water was tears, and the theological questions about the provisions of porridge, cabbage and its proper observances and times-of-day and abasements, which might yet have a bearing on them too.

There, we are getting somewhere at last, it's a step in the right direction, backwards, chewing the pith, regurgitating, only then forwards. Shade ahead, there is none, proceeding in a curve is better in such latitudes, more direct it is said. So they give you a map and tell you, ignore it, trust to your lights. Worst, cold or hot, it is such an elementary matter, you would have thought the training included the means of telling the one from the other, or of some physiological certainty that couldn't be overruled by mere cussedness, swearing it's really heat till blue in the face. It is at least bright, thanks to the divine lightswitch, ready to turn us all to statues of our former selves, when it pleases, and so hop, while there's a chance. One leg is gammy, trench foot, from the cold, or the heat, or the assault, or the sand, it is necessary to limp, even if for show, the leg tied up in a sling does nothing for circulation, the feeling is going now. It's in the blood they say. Disorders of circulation, things told by the ones who were there, or say they were, they pass it all on to you, the good, the bad, the rotten. It is my principle that I ought to repeat what is said, though I am not bound to believe it. And yet I am bound to repeat it. Which doesn't mean I don't choose to. There were my masters, it wasn't like that with them, though they are out of earshot now, we're too far back for them. Between all my memoirs the problems obtain, between all my contrivances, interest accrues to the repeated spots and the things themselves lighten and float off, they lose interest, which I cannot bear, I'll chuck out the lot, or I'll rivet them, all their rubbish. Hence this shelf, this between, my current contrivance against complete sleep, on which sleep is possible only in minutes, a perpetual waking and jerking of the neck, maintaining vigilance at all costs on the shop opposite, ready to deny it again if asked. Pigheadedly insisting on right of secession, would imply there was a union, or had been, *and so he destroys what he loves*, in order to point it, ach, we would need a proper critic for that, to find what is a game, a quick switch under the tumblers, this for that, and what merely flailing.

Hence the worry about feet and where to put them. Two back for every one forward at this rate, an odd sort of progress, even Janus would have trouble walking backwards with a bold face over a pair of buttocks. A bold face on an awkward gait. Never explained you see, how it all comes apart with the application of a little too much thoughtfulness. They just think it's enough to say Janus-faced, without asking how he walked or which side got what view. How could he walk without disturbing the sleepers, and providing proper balance for his wobbling head, it is important to tread carefully, that is all we know on the ground. Gryphons? They are asleep, they are at the edge of the map, they will never wake up, thank God, other things will, wrap your coins in cotton, cast keys in the snow, keep mum, get dad to buy you proper shoes at least, look after them, the canker will get you, the frostbite, the footrot, the worm in at the toe, stuff your boots with sage. Hot or cold, still impossible to say. A matter not reliant on hearsay like the edges of the map, it's here, now, around and in us, in our lungs, and we aren't sure if this is a coldroom or a bloody desert. I didn't see you in Malaya. I didn't see you in the jungle, doing your bit for your country, I didn't see you in Ceylon. The other people on the transport have their own worries, you hear this rigmarole so many times, it's sometimes a shout, then a mumble. But be still, the broadcast is apparently over. An attack of the fidgets, you can get down now, nearer the ground. None of which helps with the matter of gryphons or fictional first causes, they must be behind the placard somewhere, I'm not satisfied where. Behind the placard, because the goldfinch has been scraped off the front, my pretty Mordant, she is all scraped off. Revealing only the legend, in oblique sans serif, *Primogeniture created this landscape for us all to enjoy. Please leave it as you would wish to find it.* What's called a sense of humour, erected as a placard, it pales somewhat in the light. But for what it's worth, after interruptions, there were said to be gryphons somewhere near Denmark or the Polish corridor, and onelegged Arimaspians who have to hop up to the gryphons to steal their gold, according to the Turkish Greek or his Scythian contacts, running off stories on demand along with the cheap clobber. The difficulty of hopping quietly might seem insurmountable, it has to be heard to be be believed, but I don't believe they were one-eyed, patent rubbish, I vaunt my freedom to disbelieve on that point, it would be impossible to see what the hand was doing, with just one, impossible to thieve, there'd be a chink of metal. With two eyes you can shut the left, then the right, reach out the hand and measure up its movement, opening both eyes, very slowly, chink, and get something no eye on its own could see. The asymmetry of the face, in which is something open, folds out about the eyes.

You'd think we had enough booty by now, after that vanishing act, folded back at you laughing, here on what might be the northern shore. But there's always someone lagging behind, someone in the party. Some abandoned shrine to raid, nothing but a sackful of grey literature in it, and light wretches that float about, in this populous white desert.

And the proviso. You get that far in the listening without it having been explained that the desert place doesn't mean snow or stones only, it could open out at the end of an hour in darkness lying still with no fixed points, in a house at night, opening one eye, then the other, or believing both are open though they are closed, the dream of being awake, and you can control it, you make this, you choose this and its attendants, its afterimages, the shapes behind the eyelid, refusing to settle, lacking most a horizon, a ledge, for all that it is insisted on. Desert without des res, supplies is extra, gardening all in, you just want a lodgement, at least for the eye, there is not even any distance but all is folded back at you, you get a giant beerbottle. They call that charity, it tastes like petrol. How to have a shelf in a desert, to set out your pieties, it would have to be portable, arranged in the evening, packed up in the morning, doubles as a workbench, it's desperate, bits would be lost undoubtedly, picked up by the gardeners, they'd bring them to you, being helpful souls. The gardeners have been with me a while now, I didn't mention them, they come and go hoeing the odd thistle, turning the odd lump of moss, for their goat which they keep at a distance, fortunately, I fear its letterbox eyes. Nobody pays them, they want nothing, fortunately, they must live hereabouts. They ought to inspire hope or some religious sentiment but appear merely uninterested, one said with some sort of spite, I don't know where he had it from, that the flowers were not flowers, merely a kind of coloured leaf. The bastard, I think I shall kill him.

And then the gardeners, the cunning portable shrine, the petrol taste are all willed below the horizon again, turbulence expected, or the horizon rose up and got them, the clouds were cliffs of ice all along, all glows with interior cold, there is darkness and a need of holds for the slow downward turn of the wheel. Stillness, ah, stillness, don't believe it though you think you must, dead nature, and with all due reluctance, Mr Chair, what did they teach you at school, concerning gravity about the poles, the tilt of the earth, the latitude, the transpolar drift, not to mention the bending of starlight, the possibility, however remote, of magnetic inversion. For that downturn you batten down the hatches and wait for spring. You need not a mascot, not an object, but a hand to suck, your own, another's, an enemy's, just so long as connected at the wrist. The man-magician's would do. He has not ever vanished, he can be roused, he is the first definite failure we have encountered, marked, I want to say on the brow but more likely by bruising on the upper arm, those ungrateful boys, there was some slip-up in the triage room, he has yet the shoulders for it, he is lightening, be quick. So suck his hand, it is no sweeter an act for the fact that he needs it too. An embrace in which who holds whom against, at least, a mutually feared which. A last triangulation in the dark, to name names, for the dark is held in this embrace of three, we are waltzing out of the picture now, and you do not disdain the puncture of bristles against the neck, there is moreover the mercy of not seeing the eyes, you make him speak, try to squeeze a word out of him, he does understand but you can't hear the voice, you fall on his neck again, it seems urgent at this juncture, but the form of words cannot be retained, that is forbidden, you cannot take them back with you, they are at the least subject to hefty duty-payments. And considerable doubt remains as to whether he said anything at all, his voice was ever soft and gentle. After which a faked new calm, recall disturbed. All resolves into the fixtures, the shelf in its reliable whiteness, spanned with toys, stones, the part-eaten meal, the box of nail parings, slipper limpets, acorn cups, swept clean at a stroke, always new, re-made, winking, a little longer yet. The hardness attracts, there's a promise of measurement if the eyes could but face it, drop a vertical, a promise of order and ranking, though the effect of concentration half obliterates the ensnared souvenirs which we must now go through carefully, the modesty they said would vanish if stared at, that which floats, by which something might be admitted, asymmetry, the fidgets, hold onto them all, the uncomforts, because they indicate an undecided nature that is neither here nor gone, mine nor yours, it looks forward too in pictures, there are shades in fidgeting, as in a squint, someone could tell me that he was compelled to come and yet he attends, and I knew him by his fidget, his hopping gait, his figment of solitude turned in the voice.

Smiling at or with then? A bland choice. It would be an error, in all this night talk, the lighting is yet fluorescent, to believe any of the aforementioned popped up out of their own will, they take the form of chance and I set about immediately to deny it them, they must simply obey the summons, which indicates how they are to go about their work, I mean mine. They laugh as they obey me, the insolent boys, skivers, what do they see at my back? Some new reveille. The dawn hour, so longed for, to end quickly, some mustering. Rays bent by the lens of air, making the house a camera; the residual superstition of motes. Matutinal folly wishes away the night too soon they said, their last saying for the present. Thaw is the order of the day – strike the ground – and then glut.

Pick up sticks then. How wide can the eyes open? That they might, that they do even unsteadily recollect, possess themselves before us, take it all on. Studying the ground, sanguine in floods.

Halicarnassos-Bodrum-London, 1993-4

Ian Hunt lives in London. He has been widely published in the visual arts press and is active as a publisher through the imprint *Alfred David Editions*.

LONG POEMS

GRAHAM FULTON

DREW MILNE

Normal Appetites

amplifications & developments
on overheard conversations

Graham Fulton

1

Stand too fast
and see stars
in the daytime.
Busy bursts of light,
Universes being born,
exquisite in
their uselessness.
Hot blood blitzing
to the head,
everything not
the way it was, everything
out of balance.
Pulse.
Fragile veins
beneath the surface.
Pints of life,
existence, pain.

The smallest things,
biggest things
that you can think of.
Suns, corpuscles.
Birth canals, canals of Mars,
not what they seem,
skin bits, dust,
each line on
the palm of
your hand.
Everywhere, nowhere.
Far too many

to count, you'll spend
the rest of your time.
Every mouthful,
heartbeat, kiss.
Every human face
is unique.
Fucking amazing,
fucking dumb,
glorious in
our pointlessness.

2

Beans in a roll,
I bought it, hungry.
Protein, energy, dripping sauce.
I've had fancy dinners before.
Lobster.
This was something else.
Soft.
Hot. My fingers
and a cool breeze on
the back of my neck.
I know how to indulge myself,
resurrect those
feelings left.

Resplendent on
a big yellow bin
outside the café
over the road.
Plastic, hard, defensive space.
People looked
as they walked past.
Fuck them,
that's what it's all about.
Red juice,
a special occasion.
Small excitements
are what you need
to make a worthless life
worthwhile.
Heinz.

I'll remember alright,
heaven for a reasonable price.

3

Striped for war,
belligerent stance.
The biggest spider
in the world.
A hairy fucker with fangs
and legs, female of course,
not into confrontation
but not a pacifist, just
guarding the nest
from painted pygmies
dancing round her,
prodding with sticks,
making her angry, grinning,
jabbing, dodging
poison, grabbing her legs,
lifting and throwing her into a pot,
cooking her, eating, dousing
the flames, knowing
they could
die any time.

Oblivion
just a scratch away.
Wild. Mental.
What a laugh.
Ordinary blokes the same as us.
Savage bastards have got it sussed,
they always go for the woman.
Devour.
Take a chance, walk a tightrope,
don't give a toss.
Cool as fuck.

4

It's all in the mind,
I just have to think.

Extravagant isn't
the word.
Think.
Doing it this way,
doing it that.
Fingers and nipples,
teeth and tongues,
yoghurt in my belly button.
Fruits of the forest,
repressed passion. Think.
Exotic foodstuffs. Think.
Precious moments,
primeval swamp,
it's in the head,
I have to.

Think.
Millions of brain cells
swimming in space.
Putting energy
into perspective,
rationalising
horny thoughts.
Forget it.
Just think, that's all
I do. The way I am.
Not much else.
Yoghurt and id.
True love, oh yes.

5

She's on telly
strutting around,
not much on, a little ride,
whipping the groin boys
into a frenzy,
singing her latest
Top Ten hit, tribal drums,
some fucking shite.
Then all of a sudden -
Bam. It went.
Right on in at breakneck speed,

the speed of fucking light.
A camera, up
her red meat tunnel, like
something from an abattoir.
Sick.

Holes.
We're full of stupid holes.
Nothing to stop fear
pushing in, out of nowhere.
Space.
Some
things weren't meant
for human consumption.
Fucking clever the way it was done.
Trick photography, mirrors, drugs.
The offspring of a screwed-up mind.
Like something. Christ,
right on up. An abattoir.

6

There's not enough
for all I want.
Space.
Fingers down the throat,
out it comes, over the pavement.
Go tonight, lie face down in
the magic gutter, moonlit pool.
Wife at home, kids in bed.
Making space, creative process.
Lovely lager, whisky chasers,
generous measures.
Not enough.
Two digits down the throat,
everyone in their proper
place.

The stars spin.
My mates are the same,
have what it takes
for a great night out.
Talk of the time
we touched this girl.

She was walking,
began to run.
We started thumping.
The wives, the kids.
Kept on going, went for it.
Hard. Men.
The way we are.
Normal.
Space, there's not
enough. Space.

7

The beautiful
slow journey of
the bat through
air, bone, brain.
Soul.
More alive than the rest.
The stomach, show them
we've got the stomach.
Take a team,
kick fuck out their faces.
Kick. Fuck.
Children of winter.
Clocks go back
at the end of October.
Boot,
half-brick snug in the hand,
the joyful swing
of the baseball bat.
The stomach,
kick in the stomach.

Something
growing,
bursting, ancient
soon to be born.
Nature. Human. Longings
older than time,
explosions of souls, desires,
windows, passers-by.
We have the power
to take it away.

What was living
is now.
Not.
Get ourselves
in touch with nature.
Kick, fuck.
Out our heads.

8

A tooth.
I took a bite,
heard it crack.
A cucumber sandwich
for lunch.
I spat it
into the basin.
Rotten, black,
lonely
in that white.
A falling away.
A thread of blood.
No pain, a surprise.
The soul, spark, whatever
you want to call it.
Wrap it
tight in tissue,
keep it in a drawer.

You'll
soon forget
the hunger you knew.
The hole seems huge
when you test with
your tongue.
It's all in the mind,
remember to tear
your heart in two,
be very normal.
Normal.
Lessons are there
to be learned.
Keep away from cucumber,
keep away from everything.

Aggropolis

Drew Milne

'The spoliation of the Church's property, the fraudulent alienation of the state domains, the theft of the common lands, the usurpation of feudal and clan property and its transformation into modern private property under circumstances of ruthless terrorism, all these things were just so many idyllic methods of primitive accumulation. They conquered the field for capitalist agriculture, incorporated the soil into capital, and created for the urban industries the necessary supplies of free and rightless proletarians.' Karl Marx

Rampart of early kin
gdom, lamp hand can
no more surly, but as
worsted lands decry to
most governable parcel,
as to wold civil squall
aurochs abound in not
them as wont, carse noy.

Thane & carls & carline
willing able fief reivers,
rangers of their dogger
lone crust to derby stars,
so vassal span to glass
in minor modes, what
diffuse trickles burn own
grands off of apex argot.

Arrant? I nearly lost my
half heid shantil shining
though the lame is way,
which than mune is worth,
bang clannish as but kin

could no more grip fringe
than teeth rankles mak a
moment too too cramasay.

Coronach the mak undid
in cordial griddle burns,
a sack of sword firing to
a river's rough wooing,
so tending extremities
whereunto ye may reach
ample scarcement, fuse
crux to steelbow now.

This too, too barren pit
y gallows, rough shod
rise do plunge back all,
semper strong to bake
o local magnate, corbie
conner, flox, manrents,
a chisel home none durst
taste so striving sunders.

But from our throat band
each one to boaster skull
a whole brood bought and
sold for some quiet death,
there native shafts to serf
through keen run pestilence,
a third off all churl, a dirt
canker of lank blown land.

Exceeding cruel, mingle
speir hemmed in to style
as a boot on other foot
loose felt a margret rose,
a taxi, mum, what wedge
there calling asserts its
ainmaist equilibrium as
a fringe now all to burn.

Back a hammer lens do
great jessie smithereens
to bolster bless arraign,
not prickle state of mars
in ready armour wards,
auld antonine crumbles
haps in rage to ditches
farflung een to danzig.

Renegades saw broke
men go, the going is
sure primogeniture to
a trace of shedding so
seldom sacked in old
sense or auld kail dosh,
said but spelt like read
lays never said fer awe.

Negleck nocht but to flee
curls oer seas, oer muling
chiel clock, the never ripe,
that seat of leanning curve
to whey & splinter grey,
vehement against idols,
caw, caw mid a grave, a
set fair but for the grace.

Brethren mort dues cure
soul fonts, hook & crook,
a took fire noblesse oblige,
piety so mother smothered
in wanton cloth dochters
to seed a tipping bath but
whipped up rabble beefy
gin bondage of strangers.

Largely dead letters shine
heretic forth & kale stunt,
bell bent on fleeter dash
as caress but tools o rift

to sun amok gaunt cries
as jasus and no quarter,
severed sore, a rip stone
to flounders blue in print.

Thorns out of pulpit be
the luggis lurid knuckle,
pillory and darling dross
under vane and fruitful
stool, fouls no flesh but
durst no pool of handfast
where but sent fine section
shocks fall, wave or crow.

Wish art burns a stake,
owl to dawning oar, so
little prophets its gale,
galley dusk welt scarry,
civil rapture & salve tar
to jeopard lives in ash,
heart singing apostatic,
a force of law, a mass.

Doth corn among chaff
rest except thou repent,
o monstiferous empire,
we espy not the flame,
decks above thy skin
coats death did so enter,
ensign chant of circe
in thy hot displeasure.

Linen & skins ring back
a swell pitch to mix some
shewe of civilitie, these
other alluterlie barbares,
no civil plant in roomes,
sic colonists then drive
a wedge between celts,
kintyre bludie to antrim.

Clamp fro plangent isle
to plantation of ulster,
laity tree carbon bound,
as thou o lord onely art
deservedly more master
than my sel, who would
had lesse been affected
in irelands & sad estate.

Gall vinegar of falsity
and contempt with the
cups of my affliction,
cyclopick monster as
fears utter extirpation,
tenants in battle array,
true banditti reappearing,
barrel o brandy on staff.

Beyond a head dyke, all
as round a rough bone,
rig torn so weedy baulk,
neer moves a mountain
diffuse in clachan haze,
seeks oatfowl eenbright,
pristine mid light wattle
going to but blank stane.

Struck dearth murrain so
to blooding the laird's ky,
visage scorn. as for want
some die, a wayside flux
shifts its flaming ague,
plague in a white cloud,
flea daunce o black rat
lays on of partly waste.

Glade poverty turns light,
stood on brink of great
jenny & water frame &
mule & throstle carding

engines gin scurvy blest,
potato mirth akindling,
a cruel havoc dauncing
thro kail & leaf & croup.

Marks of tide, a radical
wash hung liberty high,
dreg silver in our cups
as no sanguine rabble,
no sir, nor a down tool
to turkey-red dyes, tar
to coal, naphtha starch
wearing veins of jasper.

Canals into the drill of
the lag, rolls so rent to
cast transplants, stook
bitter on summit entails
their tapering heads do
cut and turn, flail sabre
in shag dragoons, your
virgin heart so burning.

What a way to cast clods
on kindred spirits, there
the sulk is on, you take it
all in, and chew mildew
like there's no wake left
and no worm, each head
of jawfall in calm lore as
so forth serries this waif.

But hither, crash viol,
the loose twang in gas
and halter, its sermon
ever falters, never no
fine tooth in sundries,
schmo labrets, there's
hurt to your elbow, so
gone on open mouths.

The taint of the carving
is in the slummy blood
of what grows feebler
in sulky grace, miasma
riding over, getting out
while the going is bad,
so less of that colossal
cheek & maiming sou.

Stark & stacked so bitter,
what crocks of shedding
on a tide of nails, pins,
even to base metals and
no end of toil, no don't
go on, leave off, hunger
to a rage, buried in bone
shackle to palpable scar.

Worse is come under in
inclement skies, before
each dark spit takes you
to water felt upon awes,
dusts down in pig iron,
swan of arc-light, flock
done to sparry feather,
ember gorse in dolefuls

In wet soil, crisp white
scale holds to its mire,
what drip stalks, such
cut swathes, the rumble
slump and insert larks,
its best lie deep, steady,
the number dogs do lay
a dirt trail in each script.

Blue moon on fed day,
smiles so still, or soon
dies, drops a halo, hot
suits of nuclear electric

on th'ensanguined suns,
garb o grime, in rails of
bleached bondehede, no
ash of its worth or page.

O fucked city, its agon
lustre in foamy rind, to
do so soft with then on
acrylic afternoons, our
one good eye flowering
me with disaffections,
ah mine hurt, it shrinks
from less, it shrugs on.

As bake or dearth into
star cot, let's lie lower
love, let's lie low until
no dark so comfortless
blight of agent can still
wager head aginst our
rotting core, as they do
expatiate of this or fall.

Have you left my ear to
locks, a field of night in
the mine, ivresse as this
hair kindles into meteor
or blows of die, a mark
as fur or as sark blisters
rent asunder, its moral
streaks in fiery blesses.

So flower the baby for
pure boot and spur, to
list with zeal on banner
sky, each bright light is
you, for the taking, our
surfing oxide, treats of
burnished ore, its civil
song so shiney in wax.

You stand on a floor
of noise, its broken
vessels turning to a
savage lavender, the
soles flying through,
as so stuns a face to
unfold in each nerve,
each slice that carves.

In strokes or gritted
hate, its proud beats
to your darker pulp,
so steer a stern, clear
out this dormant sky,
now so cool or crost,
and cut a dash, esprit
doux, out of all cry.

Drew Milne was born in Edinburgh in 1964. In Autumn 1995 he was the first Writer in Residence at the Tate Gallery, London. He lectures in English at the University of Sussex. Recent books of poetry include *Sheet Mettle* (1994) and *Carte Blanche* (1995)

LOST POETS FOUND

ANDREW GREIG

RON BUTLIN

BRIAN McCABE

'... and this is the "A" string...'
Jim Campbell, Andrew Greig, Jim Hutcheson, Ron Butlin, Brian McCabe – in the recording studio at Barclay Terrace (where The Rezillos' 'Can't Stand My Baby' was recorded) in 1976.

Horns & Wings & Stabiliser Things

Fairly reliable memories of 'The Lost Poets'

Andrew Greig

IT COULD BEGIN in George Square at *Poem 72*. That festival was a piece of its time – a one day Happening running at three venues simultaneously at Edinburgh University with 22 Scottish poets, a lecture-performance on concrete poetry by Edwin Morgan, a multi-media event from his 'Warhol period' that still makes Ron Butlin blush, an exhibition of Ian Hamilton Finlay, and an audience of a thousand. It was my first public reading. I was 20, had had a poem in the *Weekend Scotsman* like Norman MacCaig, and my hand was shaking and sweating so badly I kept dropping my typed sheets. At that point I decided it would help to carry some of the poems in my head and have the page as a disposable prop. I still do this.

In the upstairs hospitality suite in the David Hume Tower MacCaig, Sorley Maclean, Robert Garioch, Edwin Morgan, Iain Crichton Smith and Sidney Goodsir Smith were making inroads into the whisky. Brian MacCabe, whom I'd only recently met and held in some awe because while still at school he'd read at the Traverse with Pete Brown and Alan Jackson, and he *had a booklet coming out – Goodbye Schooltie – (This title embarrasses me now*: B.M.) had to point out who was who. They were too old and eminent for us to talk to, and whisky wasn't really our thing, so we nipped down to the basement for a quick smoke. On the way we bumped into a loud, cheerful person. Her name was Liz Lochhead and she was apparently looking forward to her first public reading ('I was terrified, Andy, just terrified'). She suggested – and this I've never forgotten – I just have fun. I was astonished that she could suggest such a thing. Making an arse of yourself in public, exposing your heart, under-developed mind and scarcely-existent technique – *fun*?

It was Ron Butlin's first reading too. He rushed and blurted through his poems. His introductions consisted of 'This is a poem'.

from Edinburgh University's *Student* magazine, 1973.

Butlin, McCabe, Greig, Lochhead – reunion bash

'This is another poem', 'This may be a poem'. I sweated and stammered through mine. I remember wittering on about salmon netting on the Tay – establishing my manual labour credentials and getting a response, almost a laugh – then going on in a high to the poem itself. Only it wasn't. It was a completely different poem I'd written two days before and at a glance made no sense to me at all. A frantic whizz through the handful of poems showed I'd left the salmon behind. Going to have to work at this, I thought.

Ron and I, now old comrades-at-arms, went on to see Brian in action. In baggy black breeks, vivid red braces, wire-rimmed glasses and a lot of Dylan hair, he ran to the front of the room and jumped directly onto the stage, cracked two jokes and three short surreal poems (or perhaps the other way round, it was hard to tell the difference in those days) and had the audience in his hand. He finished, shouted 'Thank you – and goodnight! Good morning! Goodbye!' and ran out the door. (*I don't remember doing this, but it may be true*: B.M.) Liz too turned out to be a natural performer and her reading was picked up in two of the reviews we pretended to be not very interested in the next day.

The day was punctuated by power-cuts that turned readings into candle-lit seances. Heath was struggling with the unions and was fairly obviously going to lose. My political friends thought him an arch-friend of the far Right, a sinister fascist. (They hadn't seen anything yet.) The week before the Trotskyites called everyone out over a 1p rise in the price of a coffee in the DHT basement. Yup, it was a golden age, though we didn't recognize it at the time: a time when the NHS and the Education system more or less worked and were free, when Election manifestoes tried to outbid each other on the number of Council houses they were going to build, when unemployment was thought to be scandalous and society-threatening at half a million. When student grants (though we never admitted it) were adequate and you could sign on through the holidays. It was effectively still part of the Sixties. Long long time ago, another world.

Brian and I had another joint in the dark loo (*I don't think so, though we may have done* B.M.) so missed Edwin Morgan's lecture (we couldn't have got in anyway, it was packed out and they were turning people away). After humiliating us at his multi-media show where at randomly-selected moments we had to stand in front of a split-screen in near-darkness and read fragments against ever-more random film-and-slides, Ron asked us to play football in the Meadows (*Not on this occasion, I don't think!* R.B.), but I stayed on to watch MacCaig and Garioch and to discover that 'the old guys' were incredibly good performers who seemed to revel in the exposure that had come to them late in their lives. They were starting to do readings more than once a year, Garioch had a book in print, *Scottish International* would interview them, there was even talk of setting up a degree course in Scottish Literature, though that was hard to imagine. Garioch was a small, round man with an expression at once humorous and slightly sad. When I felt able to speak to him he told me that in the old days he and the other poets mostly sent wee poems to each other in letters. And he called the booklet *Seventeen Poems For Sixpence* that he'd done with Sorley Maclean 'basically vanity press'. He looked round the excited gathering and picked up his glass. 'It's awfy different noo ...'

Next year's *Poem 73* was even bigger with an audience of some 1,500 and MacDiarmid packing out the 600 seater George Square Theatre, but it was the first one that mattered. With the SAC's Writers in Public and Writers in Schools schemes yet to be set up, there were very few public readings. A get-together on this scale astonished and energised everyone. For us it was a landmark. Three of us did our first readings there. We first met as performers there. Out of it came the first book I'd been in – *7 New Voices*, with Liz and Brian – and then John Schofield went on to print (high-tech electric typewriter) *White Boats* with myself and Catherine Czerkawska. The first collection, getting a start, is the hardest.

And the friendship and mutual encouraging and criticism and influencing between the four of us started there. It showed there really was a constituency for poetry. When we did dare talk to Grand Old Men (and they were all men), they were open, friendly, encouraging, ready to help out with references and sponsorship for bursaries, and always remained so. The message was that there was room at the bar, that you could be serious about writing but never brag or posture.

Ron, Brian and Liz might disagree, but I felt while listening to the Grand Old Men talk and flyte and reminisce, that we were being subtly initiated, that there was a *constituency*, an evolving tradition and an attitude, that we were open to add to. It's a great help that by and large the Grand Old Men were friends but very diverse, so they never insisted in turn that one had to conform to this school or that. (The last of the Lallans v English wars was rumbling towards exhaustion, and the best of the writers seemed to get on writing without any doctrine.)

So much follows from what came before. We took on as natural this atmosphere of friendship-in-diversity. We took on (emphasised by the ethos of the Beat and Liverpool Poets) the assumption that a poetry reading was a performance, not a lecture illustrated by a few poems. It was part entertainment. This attitude may have come from the ceilidh rather than the academic tradition. And if your poetry was serious, then at least you make the introduction light, crack a few jokes. In time Ron and myself, given that our poetry was not a bundle of laughs, sat down and deliberately wrote two funny or at least entertaining poems each (he's still using his, but claims to have written a third recently).

Since and partly because of *Poem 72*, I've seen us as *carrying on* in both senses.

Looking now at our first booklets and pamphlets (including Ron's *The Wonnerfu Warld o John Milton*, hand-scribed by Brian, photocopied, stapled, and sold door-to-door round the Pollock Halls of Residence through four editions – 'The most profitable book I ever wrote' – it's striking that only Ron used Scots then. At that time I think Brian, Liz and myself instinctively felt that writing in Scots was awkward, backward-looking, confining. It was, in a word, square. It certainly wasn't for people who had come to consciousness in the Sixties and were probably more excited by music than poetry in any case. Apart from Ron, we all body-swerved MacDiarmid for years – there was something glowering, oppressive, hectoring and authoritarian about his aura, image and pronouncements. He was around, like a distant thunder we had no desire to get closer to.

We all had varying degrees of Scots in our conversation, but didn't use it to write with. I remember occasionally finding myself writing a Scots word that came naturally, only to find it looked gey queer/very strange when typed up, surrounded by English, so I dropped it. I couldn't see how it could fit.

I was very impressed that Ron had actually read *A Drunk Man*. Perhaps because he had and recognised it was Modernist and revolutionary rather than incomprehensible or couthy, he used his Scots to write about Jimi Hendrix and warped personal-sexual relationships. That puzzled and intrigued me, though I didn't see how I could follow it. I don't recall feeling defensive or inferior or oppressed or suppressed in using (rather, not using) part of my natural language. I don't think that's why I ignored it for a while. It just didn't resonate the present or the future, it wasn't part of rock 'n roll, and it didn't fit. None of us remotely aspired to be English, or thought ourselves disadvantaged. If there was a censor, it came from inside, but I don't think that was it either.

And being from our generation, growing up with TV, films, rock music, none of us spoke a consistent, dense Scots. So it seemed phoney to put one on.

After a while, Ron ceased writing in Scots, and round about the same time Liz, encouraged by being part of the Hobsbaum-Kelman-Leonard group in Glasgow, started to find ways of using and writing Glaswegian (with, I think, some less purely urban elements). She worked out a practical solution to the spelling and accent. She was always a *voice* poet, then she acquired a way of putting that voice on the page. The early poems are written in English, but she never *read* them that way.

At that time we tended to be most excited by American and European poets: Zbiebnew Herbert, Cavafy, Apollinaire, Ed Dorn, the Beats, Miroslav Holub, Eliot, Carlos Williams. I'd glanced at Larkin and Hughes but found them dull, over-studied, literary. It was rumoured that Ron had read Auden. Of the Scottish poets I think we all agreed about MacCaig and Edwin Morgan. Eddie was *modern*. Despite his dress sense, he was definitely *with it*. He was the only one of those senior poets one could imagine having heard of The Doors or The Velvet Underground, let alone listened to them. He had range and versatility, he'd try anything, he showed that all doors were open. His poetry with its vast range of style, tone, subject, technique, its affirmative embrace of the present and the future, its refusal to be limited by notions of home versus abroad, somehow *gave permission*. And he remains the Scottish poet most frequently namechecked by the new generation of Scottish poets – an astonishing achievement, to remain a vital catalyst for thirty five years, to bridge the Sixties to the Nineties.

All our seniors had jobs. With the exceptions of MacDiarmid and Mackay Brown, they didn't live by writing. They were, in that sense only, amateurs. We didn't know then that it was possible to live – just – by writing poetry. We were the ones who had to discover that.

I tried going straight and got a job as an advertising copywriter. Neither of these lasted long. We drifted on, writing and doing whatever was necessary to be able to keep writing.

Again it comes down to social-economic conditions. This was the period of Literature on the DHSS, when it was possible to sign on without much hassle or interference. None of us or Kelman, Tom Leonard, Alasdair Gray, could have survived and kept writing without it.

When really broke I did farm work. On one occasion Ron stood in the street and added up the cost of everything he was wearing – it came to under £2. He bought everything from jumble sales. We carried on student-style, sharing flats and walking everywhere. In winter at Ron's, woolly hats and fingerless gloves and two sweaters were fairly essential. We were living short-term with no particular plans or expectations. A booklet, a reading gig, or sometimes just getting something published and paid for it – was an occasion for celebration. There was no known pattern for what we were doing. There was no structure, no circuit, no notion of a career. Sooner or later it would have to stop because We Couldn't Go On Like This. Having our dole cut off, or marriage and children, or some other natural disaster, would bring us to our senses.

Everything was provisional. We didn't know *Lanark* would be published, that Scottish Literature would become a degree course, that there would be a circuit of readings, posts, awards and bursaries, that we'd ever write another poem. In the meantime, doubtful, hopeful, *lost*, like Ron in his jumble sale trainers we scuffed by.

In April '75 perhaps we were driving in a white Beetle in a slight daze somewhere in the West Highlands. We'd been talking about setting up poetry and music readings ourselves because there were so few on offer, maybe even doing a Fringe show. In ourselves and round about us, we weren't too sure where we were and that seemed laughable. A van came round a blind corner fast, I twitched the wheel and it missed us by a coat of paint.

Brian coughed. 'We were nearly the Lost Generation of poets there.' More laughter, and thus the Lost Poets name was born, as a joke, a mockery of our mortality and our ambitions. So we'd find a venue, have our favourite writers as guests, rope in musician friends, and do a season or two of shows. By the time we got to our destination, if we ever did, we'd decided to ask Liz, whom we knew and liked and whose work we respected, if she'd like to join us. It seemed right to try to bridge the Glasgow-Edinburgh gap. It could be fun and an excuse for a few get-togethers. Perhaps we could put off getting a Real Job a bit longer.

Andrew at 28: But imagine being forty and still not having a job, that would be depressing.

Ron: Look, man, imagine being forty and *having* a job – now that really is depressing!

More laughter. Ron's conviction bohemianism was an inspiration. It was at moments like that, or arguing minutely over each other's new work, or commiserating or celebrating, that we supported and developed each other. Without that context and the sense of communality, it is easy to peter out or become cranky.

The Gender Gap wasn't significant to us. Liz was a friend, a good writer and a good performer, that's why it was obvious to involve her. Looking back we didn't succeed in closing the Edinburgh-Glasgow gap. Liz' development with the Hobsbaum-Leonard-Kelman-Gray group went on largely unknown to us. We saw only the results. It was a simple and absurd effect of logistics: 45 miles was just too far apart to share our lives. It took time and money to go from one coast to the other. At best we broke down some of the suspicions.

Probably we should have had a series of Glasgow shows, but that would have meant Liz doing most of the organization and groundwork, so it didn't happen. On the couple of occasions when we did go through to Glasgow for parties we were taken aback by the sheer volume of alcohol (which was not the drug of our choice) going down throats. Brain cells were dying in their millions. There was some interesting crack, contact was established and goes on still, but there was no doubt this was a different culture with its own groupings, preoccupations and agendas. Perhaps Alan Spence, being from the West but living in Edinburgh, and one of our first guest readers, was the only one capable of belonging in both worlds at once, and the one crucial talent everyone was affected by was Edwin Morgan.

I read solo in Glasgow at the Third Eye Centre. I was very nervous because it was my first reading from *Men On Ice* which was a very odd poem, and especially because Tom Leonard was there. Tom was said to barrack or hit people whose work he didn't like. I went on, my voice sounding more and more English and middle-class to my ears. And what wasn't English was American-tinged, like the poem itself. I had to jump up and down and do voices and wave my arms a lot. At the end Tom came up to me. I braced myself. He gripped my upper arm. 'Ed Dorn, pal! Fuckin magic!'

Saved. After Carlos Williams, Tom like myself was a big fan of Ed Dorn's 'Gunslinger' and recognized its pervasive influence on *Men On Ice*. At that time, meeting someone who'd even heard of Dorn let alone being turned on by him, was like meeting a secret brother. The gap was bridged – by a mutual admiration for an American. That's Scottish.

Largely in jest, for a while we yarned about the Lostology – a mock-Science or metaphysics, thinking of Alfred Jarry's Pataphysics. We made a sketchy attempt to develop it as a philosophical-ethical-aesthetic position (or non-position). We could see that writers, especially European writers, were constantly forming movements then throwing each other out of them. This was both appealing and ludicrous, and the Lostology was largely a parody of a movement manifesto.

Fortunately it has been lost. The only consistent thing about it.

The significant element was not so much a shared sense of no longer having fixed bearings – political, moral, role models, metaphysical certainties, beliefs religious or aesthetic – but that in the end this was something to be accepted, even affirmed, rather than mourned. Sing if you're glad to be lost. That affirmation is very much of the time that formed us, somewhere between the Existential nihilism of the Fifties and the Post Modern nihilism of now.

Under the Lost Poets umbrella, we did a season of shows at the Theatre Workshop in Stockbridge, another at the Netherbow, another at the Traverse. And two (I think) years on the Fringe. Memorable guests included Robert Garioch (one of his last readings), Edwin Morgan, Alan Jackson (in manic mode with German tin helmet, his *Listen Punk* booklet stapled with a large safety pin), Alan Spence, MacCaig, Pete Brown. Kathleen Jamie came to one of these shows and sent us a note: *Methinks I'll thump the next person who says poetry's boring*, and from then on her latest poems would be among the ones passed around for discussion and re-working. The core of the music was Jim Hutchison, who virtually became our in-house designer and illustrator of our future books. It was Jim who spray-painted a large black and white maze as a backdrop for our early productions. That maze (which doubled as a thumbprint) became a kind of logo, stood well for the Lost, and sparked off quite a lot of talk about mazes and minotaurs. I can't remember whether it was cause or coincidence, but my *Men On ice* was full of minotaur reference, Liz wrote her Ariadne Version poem and increasingly reworked myths, Brian produced a 'Minotaur Blues' which was our a finale:

> My troubles started before I was born
> My mama wis crazy, my daddy had horns,
> When I first showed up, nobody smiled,
> 'That's a crazy baby, that's a real bull child ...'

At their best, these were shows rather than separate readings. We did sit down beforehand to look for links and themes and connections. We cut between different poets and the songs, worked out links. And we did a certain amount of ensemble – we tackled HOOF from *Men On Ice* with four voices, some stamping and very skewed timing; Brian assembled a cut-up found poem called 'Here's Why' that Liz added to and we did together; there was the show-stopping (and sometimes show-disintegrating) 'Roll On', part-poem, part-song:

> *I can live I can love I can push I can shove*
> *(With my horns and my wings and my stabaliser things)*
> *I can laugh I can frown turn the tortoise upside down*
> *(with my horns & wings etc ...)*

And one more time in French:

Je peux lire je peux dire je peux mourir
(Avec mes oreilles mes corneilles et mes choses de stabalisé)

Brian wrote the best words but found it nearly impossible to come in at the times set by the beat. (*I disagree – everyone else was out*: B.M.) Liz had trouble getting there on time (waiting to see if she'd turn up at all kept us on our toes). Ron and I were reliable except when we weren't. And the band?

Ron: And now we have music from ... Jim, what are you called this week?

Jim (with the merest blush): The Great Deep.

Ron: Ah, right. And the Great Heap are going to play ... What d'you call it again, Jim?

Jim (inspecting the ceiling): Gothic Soul, Ron. It's a sort of a joke.

Ron: Oh. Glad to hear that ...

In those days we wrote only poetry. It hadn't really occurred to us to do anything else. All the Grand Old Men were poets. Archie Hind had written a novel in the Sixties, so had someone called Alan Sharp, and that was about it. One day Brian turned up and announced 'I've written a short story.' Ron and I stared at him: 'Why?' 'Don't worry.' he said, 'it's short enough for readings and it's funny.'

And it was. That was the beginning of the change. He kept writing stories until Mainstream published *The Lipstick Circus* and prose was no longer just a sideline. By this time Ron was also writing stories which eventually formed *The Tilting Room*. Liz was moving towards monologues, cabaret and sketch material. On a rare visit to Glasgow I helped Liz carry a vast bundle of handwritten manuscript to a typist. 'Short stories?' I asked. 'No, it's a play about Mary Shelley and Frankenstein.' The Lost Poets seemed to be finding themselves in other mediums.

For some years I held out. When I saw Norman MacCaig he would always enquire, as if to check I had not abandoned the True Faith, 'Still not writing *prose*, I hope?'

Eventually I succumbed on being offered advances for two prose books about Himalayan expeditions. That got me used to actually getting paid for books and to sitting on my arse for hours typing away. It satisfied a latent work ethic – unlike poetry, it could be and had to be done on a daily basis – and it communicated to a larger audience. And as you get older life seems less like a few distilled lyric moments, and more like one damn thing after another; in other words, narrative.

Now of course the majority of young writers I meet are writing novels as automatically as we once opted for poetry, and largely for the same reason: the presence of older and successful role models. They have agents, sign multi-book contracts, are disciplined, publicised and highly productive. They can actually make a living directly from writing. This is as wonderful as it was previously unimaginable.

We lived more or less in each other's pockets, sometimes borrowing from them. At various times we've shared flats and lives. In those days Ron, Brian and I would go over each other's poems virtually as they were being written. Though we wrote and write very differently, there must have been cross-influences as we argued and revised and shared, hammering out both our common principles and our different directions.

The closeness of that first ten years inevitably starts to loosen. We become busy, we live apart, we become married and/or have children. Now we are more likely to write a whole book before showing the MS to each other. It becomes harder and rarer to arrange to meet together, and it usually involves answerphones.

That's alright, that's what happens. The valuable part has been done. We've aided and abetted each other, and now we get on with it. There remains a special warmth that has its roots in the past. It is easy to be nostalgic when going over the movable feast of early days when the present was extemporized and the future was unknown and we found ourselves being happily lost.

A year or so ago I came across an old Lost Poets Bank Account left over from the Fringe. We'd ended up with a profit of £9.27. I took it to the bank and discovered that with interest we now had over £20. We agreed to close the account and reconvene for a celebratory meal with partners.

It was a fine evening. We ate and drank a good deal, stories were retold and disputed, Jim sang, we resurrected 'Horns & Wings' which was as disorganised as it had been some twenty years before. Brian had dug out 'Here's Why' and we did that together, along with bits of 'HOOF'. Photos were taken, the usual.

A good evening, I thought, stumbling home. Between us we seem to have written some twenty five books, plus Liz's plays. More important, we're all still writing, no one's dried up or given up, and we still really like each other despite the drift and changes of time. We've turned forty, we still don't have Real Jobs, and – it's much better than I'd imagined.

Bibliography
Poetry
Seven New Voices (Garret Arts, 1972)
White Boats (with Catherine Czerkawska) (Garret Arts, 1973)
Men On Ice (Canongate, 1977)
Surviving Passages (Canongate, 1982)
A Flame In Your Heart (with Kathleen Jamie) (Bloodaxe, 1986)
The Order Of The Day (Bloodaxe, 1990)
Western Swing (Bloodaxe, 1994)

Non-Fiction
Summit Fever (Century Hutchinson, 1985)
Kingdoms of Experience (Hutchinson, 1986)

Novels
Electric Brae (Canongate, 1992)
The Return of John Macnab (Hodder Headline, 1996)

That Summer: When Modernist Met Theory Queen

Andrew Greig

The flesh she sat in, like a glowing robe
worn casually to go about the world in,
required no ornament, had none.
No bangles, paints, rings, nor unguents.
So she thought and rocked that summer,
naked as virtue in the hammock
beneath the vines in broken light.
The mesh raised faint welts on her skin
as she improvised on discourse, the Other,
the text redoubled, slidey signifiers,
all that French Quarter jazz – to me,
deaf to anything but her!

> 'I love cats, causes and analysis.
> This love you urge is suspect,
> founded on the bourgeois construct
> of the individual, who as we know
> is not Mrs, Miss or Ms – but myth.
> So how can you say you love me?'

      Ah, the way she turned
sentences and her head alike
with an upward questioning turn!
She came in from the garden,
her arms full of veg
and her head full of politics,
quoting Lacan, Benjamin, Foucault,
while I chopped onions and logic.
She drove a post through a Modernist heart.
Sometimes those mealtimes brought
a little water to the eyes.

> 'But surely love obscures its object
> like a fist against the sun?
> How can you know me that way?
> This is not the way to know me.'

And whispered in the night,

   'I say *Je t'aime* – the foreign language
   because this feeling's strange to me.'

One scared to feel, the other
loath to reconsider –
through prickly days and sticky nights
we ran our summer seminar
on difference of thought and gender...

Seadh. Without her I never would have gained
this Doctorate in Higher Objectivity.
I concede feeling's no excuse, and 'love'
the slipperiest of all discourses.
Yet now,
        when all our words
make dust along the whispering gallery,
I do not give a monkey's for those thinkers.
Memory has its tides, and now waters
tilt back to thoughtless parting lips,
her serene and gracious nod that summer
as she, the theory queen, at last inclined
and head met body in the shower.

Andrew Greig was born in Bannockburn in 1951. He graduated from Edinburgh University in 1975 with an MA in Philosophy, and is now a full-time writer, living mostly in Orkney and the Lothians.

Appreciations

Brian McCabe

I READ album sleeves before I read books. I found some poetry I liked in the Penguin Modern Poets Series – a lot of European and American poets, as well as British. I first read Bukowski in that series (and his name is always followed, in my mind, by Lamantia and Norse). Closer to home: Edwin Muir, Edwin Morgan, Alan Bold and Alan Jackson. It's good that the series has been revived, because I remember that as a teenager very concerned about how to best spend the pay for my Saturday job in Halfords, getting three poets in one book seemed like a good deal. I could not afford their individual volumes – and poetry anthologies are like those old photographs of the whole school – it's hard to recognise anyone.

As a schoolboy I went to a few readings in Edinburgh, some at the Traverse Theatre in the High Street, organised by Alan Jackson and Pete Morgan. I remember Pete Morgan very vividly, both as a reader of his poems and a person who had what they call in the theatre *presence*. He was big, blond, blue-eyed, and barrel-chested, sort of ape-like in some way, yet very charming, very civilised. He sometimes made me think of Frankenstein's monster – not only in his physical demeanour, but also in his personal history, which he carried around inside him – as if he had swallowed something terrible like mercury as a child. He played rugby, smoked Embassy Regal and drank pints of beer. He also grew his hair long, smoked dope and wrote poetry. He was always on the edge between what was called straight and what was considered hip. Women seemed to find him very attractive. Fucked up by his father, a military type, Pete had been in the army for six years. Then he had gone into advertising as a copywriter.

His poems were emphatically staccato in their rhythms, and had the simplicity of songs. Some had a blues quality about them. They were advertising jingles set to the unrelenting rhythm of a punishing afternoon on the drill-ground. He looked at the audience askance as he read, as if shocked by the words he himself was speaking. The poems probed the question of what it meant to be a person in society, certainly, but they also questioned the alternative – the prevailing 'love an peace' ethos of the time. For me they dramatised the struggle to get free of imposed restrictions by others – parents and other figures of authority, but also the insidious influence of one's peers, one's friends. Above all, his poems were about the struggle to come to terms with the self.

> I change my colour for my company –
> a purple knight sees purple in my cloth
> a yellow knight sees yellow
> blue knight blue
> the blackest knights I raise my visor to.
> (from 'The Rainbow Knight's Confession')

Pete Morgan showed me the ropes about the poetry business, invited me to take part in readings, patted me on the back to quell my nerves. I think it is tremendously important for a fledgeling writer to meet someone who knows the business more and is willing to help. In a sense, the older writer is encouraging competition, and Pete Morgan was big enough in himself to do that. He got in touch with me in the first instance when an acquaintance of his had read my first published poems and had told him: 'That's poetry.' He was my mentor. He taught me how to read in public and how to be critical of my own performance, my own writing. He also gave me a great lesson as a human being, for though he didn't feel totally happy with himself and his life, he was honest with himself about this and was always questioning his own motives and behaviour as well as other people's.

Alan Jackson also struck me as someone who questioned everything – about society, about Scotland, about religion, about himself. He was a Merlinesque character, and a bit of a wit on stage. He obviously enjoyed being up there, talking to an audience directly. Some of his earliest poems were small, pointed, acid comments on deeply-rooted Calvinist restrictions:

> KNOX 1
> the old scots grim man
>   with the chin
> eats an apple on the bus
> he hides it in his pocket between bites
>   for fear of the animal
>   for fear of the people

Others were quite introspective things, and in most poems he looked both outwards and inwards. He had a healthy ego as a writer, but he questioned and undermined this in the work. As a younger writer anxious to hustle my own little poems and get myself on that stage, what impressed me most about Alan was his great belief in the power of poetry – he really did think that something you could write might change the history of Western thought completely. I think Alan felt that the world was changing radically, that poetry was part of that change. What gave his work its charge, however, was the way this change was also perceived as deeply personal – that any examination of Scotland, say, was also Alan's way of looking in the mirror.

I started to take part in some of these readings when I was still at school. I heard most poets read their work at readings before I read them on the page. Edwin Morgan, Robert Garioch, Norman MacCaig and Hugh MacDiarmid – these were poets I heard, for the most part, before I read their work in books. MacDiarmid obviously cast an enormous shadow, but at the time I am speaking about – late sixties and early seventies – I think Garioch and MacCaig and Morgan had a more immediate influence on younger writers in Scotland. At times we tried to imitate them, but they proved to be inimitable. But they still represented something of enormous importance to all of us, and each in his own distinct way. Garioch, to me, was a really droll, satirical spirit. Though his language – Scots – seemed old-fashioned (then, but not now) his poems used the speaking voice in a very engaging and humourous way, and he was always concerned with modern themes and recent developments in the world – more so than we younger poets, in fact.

MacCaig was a powerful influence over younger writers who heard him read, both as a person and a writer. What he emphasised was lucidity, the long haul to lucidity. I think this was a very healthy influence – it was as if he was saying to us: just say what you mean as clearly and simply as you can, and if you are honest and if you are clever, that is enough. Of course, MacCaig exemplified something which was inimitable. A MacCaig poem is a MacCaig poem, and could not be mistaken for anything else. That is not a comment on the merit of the poetry. One could say the same of work by Tom Leonard, Jim Kelman, Liz Lochhead, Edwin Morgan, Iain Crichton Smith, Alan Spence and many other Scottish writers. I remember MacCaig saying that when you read the Scottish magazines you knew who you were reading, but if you read the English magazines you could change the names around and it wouldn't make any difference. At the time, he was certainly right, though perhaps this was not a comment on merit either. In any case, MacCaig's sensibility was impossible to ignore.

Morgan had an equal influence, but different: he was, and still is, highly adventurous in his writing. His work said to me: anything is possible in a poem, there is absolutely nothing a poem can't deal with. Having said that, in a certain way his work was perhaps too concerned with social and scientific realities to be escapist enough for the prevailing social outlook of the seventies, though I think he enioyed and welcomed the tolerance and optimism of that period. Like Pete Morgan, Edwin Morgan struck me from the first as an extraordinary reader of his work – but the work was uppermost, not the person. The person had, somewhere along the line, become sacrificed to the work. When you heard him read, it was as if the poem itself was speaking through this unlikely medium in a suit and tie and sideburns.

Tom Leonard was also enormously influential – again, no one tried to write like him, or if they did, they didn't publish it – because he had made certain things uniquely his own. He did give me one of the best pieces of advice I've had from an older writer: never apologise for something you are about to read. Even if you can't remember why you wrote the fucking poem in the first place, there is nothing worse for an audience than being told that what is about to follow isn't, in the author's opinion, all that great.

When I first heard Liz Lochhead read I felt a real excitement – the word is not too strong – and it was the dense, clever, rhythmic stretching and bending of language which excited me. She was making poetry include things it hadn't included before: she was developing a new vocabulary of very specific brand names alongside a strongly Scottish quirkiness, but there was also an emotional depth in her poetry, which was the thing that really hooked me. There was absolutely no doubt in my mind that what she was doing in her poetry was completely new. The fact that she was one of the very few women writing and publishing and appearing in public at this time also gave the work a very strong edge.

Although Liz was very much exploring a woman's point of view in her work, there was nothing by a male writer which dealt with relationships so honestly and so thoroughly. So it seemed to me that she was very much writing about me and my relationships, and she was the only writer who was doing that, for me, in Scotland. She was also a very committed reader of her work – funny, entertaining, and profound.

The Lost Poets is a kind of footnote to the above. I think Andy Greig was the only one of us who took it seriously as a kind of 'school', and even so his 'lostology' was, I think, largely tongue-in-cheek quasi-aesthetics. Andy was always at work on highly ambitious sequences – someone with a novelist's mind writing poetry. He was always highly energised about the shows, and I think he got a tremendous buzz from performing.

My own view is that The Lost Poets had its origins not in any ideological or philosophical concurrence between its protagonists, but in a very practical need to stage readings in Edinburgh. That was all that it was about really, a few people of roughly the same age getting semi-organised and putting on a show. There were some terrible nights and some good nights. We provided a platform for others, including older writers, and writers younger or even less established than us. To that extent I think it served a useful purpose.

It also provided a platform for Ron Butlin. Though Ron was and still is a powerful reader of his work, the poetry was dense, mystical, laconic and profound – in other words, kind of difficult for the average audience. But I think that getting up and reading this extraordinary stuff – some of which I think Ron himself only understood on a subliminal level – was good for him, and in fact he came to terms with an audience through The Lost Poets readings.

For me, it was all enormously enjoyable. I loved the readings, and hearing the others read their work – and the music was actually of a very high standard compared to what you often heard at readings in those days. Jim Hutcheson seemed to be the only constant factor in a band which changed its personnel and its name from reading to reading.

There is something tremendously exciting about giving a new work its first airing to a live audience – especially if you discover that people enjoy it, and that communication is possible through writing. That's the great thing, that amazing buzz you feel when you read something fresh and it works.

When I was in Canada, people were surprised by the fact that poets of my generation in Scotland knew and read and were in touch with the older generation of Scottish writers. Conversely, it seemed to me to be a lamentable thing that in Canada there wasn't this communication between the generations going on. Most of the poets I met were doing their own little thing and were very aware of what was being published by whom and who had won the Governor General's Award for Literature and who hadn't, but they hadn't read Douglas Le Pan. Whether or not they would like Douglas le Pan or identify with his poetry is besides the point. What bothered me was that they had a blind and mindless faith in the new – or rather, the current – but were ignorant of what had gone before. If this was Scotland, I kept telling myself, these younger poets would be making a point of calling Le Pan up, visiting him at midnight, and finding out how things were in his day. As we have done here – especially, perhaps, with MacCaig.

And he is not the only one with that tolerant and intrigued attitude to the young upstarts. Edwin Morgan, Crichton Smith, Sorley MacLean, Alasdair Gray, George Mackay Brown – the list could go on for a shortish paragraph – they have always been equally interested in and concerned about the future of Scottish literature. There is communication and appreciation between the generations of writers here, and that is an invaluable thing.

I met Tom Leonard recently, and he told me that one day he heard a programme about the New Scottish Poetry on Radio Scotland. Two or three New Scottish Poets were interviewed. At the end of it, the presenter said: 'So, the future of Scottish Poetry is in safe hands, then?' All of them concurred. 'God Forbid!' cried Tom Leonard – and let's hope it isn't.

Bibliography
Spring's Witch (Mariscat, 1984)
The Lipstick Circus (Mainstream, 1985: reprinted 1988, 1990)
One Atom to Another (Polygon, 1987)
The Other McCoy (Mainstream, 1990: Penguin, 1991)
In A Dark Room With A Stranger (Hamish Hamilton, 1993: Penguin, 1995)

Six Poems

Brian McCabe

A Father

As you cram your mouth
with some very earthly delights,
your golden hair shines, like
plucked harp-strings in the light,

That is called a simile.

In your skin's glow is
the apparition of fruit.
Your hesitant confidences are
the cries of extinct birds.

A couple of metaphors.

Angel, come and sit on my knee,
hear your father's sour words
as he savours your sweetness:
'Repeat after me: never

accept similes or metaphors
from strangers.'

Innocence

At ten, I was taut how two spel
by a roothless, sadistick Mr Townshend.
His name had a silent haitch.
And he belted us and belted us
when we coud not spel *admonish*.
Sadistick with a sad i and a stick.

Every day was a long list of words
I had to spel my slow way threw.
Leter by leter. From memery.
Evrey one in order. Alowd.
I rimember titerope-walking my way
to the middel of the word *innocence*,
in no sense noing what it ment
or what came nixt – 'sinse' or 'sence'.
And I fell, then felt the rong hend
of Townshend's sad, sadistick stick.
But, after schewl, in the pleygrund,
I saw Townshend, his wyfe, theyre new baybe.
I hunderstood what hinnocence ment then.
That baybe, moutheng vuiwoels, staered it me
with eyes fool of it, and I thoght:
youll lern to put your i befour you're c
hexept when it comes hafter your e.

From *The Big Sister Poems*

1. A Message

Wee brither Ah'v come wi a message fur ye.
No fae Santa naw –
it's fae Da.
Lissen wull ye.

See before you goat boarn
see Da still hud a joab tae do.
Used ta get bacon n eggs fur wir breakfist.
Ma used tae could afford tae get a hair-do.

Nen she goes an gits pregnant again.
An even allo it wis bi axydent
Da said wi could mibbe still ufford it.
He ment you.

Turns oot wi cannae.

Thither hing is
this room before you came along
only hud the yin bed in it.
Mine.

See there isnae really room fur the two.
So what wi yin hing an anither
an since you wir the last tae arrive
Da says youve tae go wee brither.

Here's yer bag its packed reddy
wi yer Beanos yer pajamies an a few
biskits fur whin ye get hungry
Ah'm sure ye'll be better oaf whiriver

ye end up so good luck an
goodbye.

2. Bedtime Story

Thir wis this boatle wi a dream in it.
Da drained it dry – fur why?
Cause this dream made everyhin seem
a loat bettur thin they wis.

A borin wurd sounded clivirer
an sortae like it mite mean more.
Even his jokes sounded funnyer
thin they ever been before.

The dream it made Da swagger
an laff and swig some more
till swagger turned intae stagger
an laff turned intae roar.

Then the dream turned intae a bad dream
an it made Da curse an swore.
So when he gets hame at last
well he slammed the frunt door.

See Da in this dream is sumbudy
who kens when he's always rite
so when Ma went an argued wi him
they sweer an shout an fite.

They fite aboot Da an his dreamin
see then the nitemare goes on.
He's hittin her an she's screamin –
this mornin Ma's upped an gone.

An Da says he cannae rimembur
whut the dream wis aw aboot.
So he goes oot tae look fur her.
Dinnae ask me how Ah fund this oot.

Ah'm yer big sister ament Ah.
Ah ken hings you dinnae that's aw.
Like the story o the boatle wi a dream in it.
A dream called aye that's rite

Get tae sleep.

3. The Lesson

Tell ye whut wee brither –
Ah'm gonnae teach ye sumhm
ye'll nivurivur furget.

Ye go haufwye up the stairs rite.
Ye turn roond ye shut yer een rite.
Ye keep yer een shut tite rite.

Noo on the count o five
Noo Ah want ye tae jump.
Noo is that clear?

Dinnae wurry wee brither.
Ah'll be staunin it the boatum here
tae catch ye so be brave.

One, two, three, four ...
FIVE Ah said Ah'd teach ye sumhm.
this is it dinnae trust enybudy.
When yer aulder ye'll thank me fur it.

Aw shut up.

Thousand Forced to Flee Disputed Region

You have read the paper too you know
The story of the thousand forced to flee
Their disputed region though no doubt
The thousand called it something else
Such as home for example here
No it did not say what forced them
Nor whether they were forced to go
Together towards the same unknown
Or to scatter as insects do
When their stone is lifted I imagine
They had time to round up the kids
Take their old if not infirm maybe
A cherished horse a particular goat
The dogs would no doubt follow
After all they were the thousand
And would pack what food they could
A bag of apples tipped from a bowl
A live chicken or two a t.v. dinner
What about the t.v. what about the radio
Leave them what have they ever done

For us take that amulet this ribbon
Those plates cups spoons a good knife
Whatever can be crammed into the pram
On the roofrack in the wheelbarrow
Of necessity it can't be much not much
Our time is short our warning brief
We ourselves don't know where to go
And the question how to get there
Will have to be answered on the way
We must flee and keep on fleeing
Until the day you open your doors
And find us standing there and say
You must be the thousand come in
We have read about you take a seat
Stay here make yourselves at home
Until you get your disputed region back
That doesn't happen though does it
We have read the paper too we know

Brian McCabe was born in 1951. He grew up in Bonyrigg, King's Lynn and Falkirk, and began writing poetry shortly before leaving Falkirk High School in 1969. After leaving university he worked in a variety of situations before becoming a self-employed freelance writer in 1980, when he was awarded a writer's bursary by the Scottish Arts Council. He presently lives in Edinburgh with his family.

The Lost Poets

Ron Butlin

AS I REMEMBER IT, The Lost Poets were formed by Brian McCabe, Andrew Greig and myself as a way of making some money, selling some books and pulling women. In none of these were we particularly successful. We invited Liz Lochhead along for glamour, and because we liked her and her work.

For five years or so we read regularly in three-week stints in the Edinburgh Fringe Festival (The Traverse, Theatre Workshop, Netherbow Theatre, etc.) plus twice-a-month winter shows at various venues in Edinburgh and elsewhere (i.e. one in Dumfries). Audience numbers ranged from three to eighty; guest readers ranged from well-known writers to well-off-the-scale bammers ("I write mostly about umbrellas', and the ilk). Some of them were sober. We gained confidence in talking to an audience, when we had one, in reading our work aloud and, most of all, in 'listening' to the house – the real secret for a speaker. On bad days I would introduce the members of the audience to each other.

Generally, the better their work the better the guests conducted themselves. We were privileged to enjoy the best education possible watching the performances of Edwin Morgan, Sorley MacLean, Alan Jackson et al at close quarters. It was extraordinarily generous of them to appear with such lowlife hopefuls as ourselves. Almost without exception the established writers were supportive and tolerant – when I introduced Peter Porter as coming from England he just smiled and gently corrected me: 'from Australia via England'.

There were, of course, one or two prima-donnas. The stage is in a different time zone from the stalls, and time passes more slowly down there – ten stage-minutes can feel like thirty or more in the hard seats. We learned how to haul them off when they dramatically overran; eventually we learned how to haul them off tactfully. One easy lesson: when the overrunner pauses for breath start clapping, and walk onto the stage saying how good it was thank you, still clapping loudly – the audience will join in, believe me. On the day several seven-minute slots would be filled by hopefuls usually more unknown even than us. These aspirants had to be

strictly monitored – there was ourselves to consider as well as the audience – Dickens's Silas Wegg, remember, used to charge extra for poetry because 'it weakens the brain'. When it came to the smooth running of an event we had to act quickly. Our opening day in the Taverse bar was brought slightly to a complete standstill by the peripatetic cigarette-machine man's insistence that he empty the cash and restock his machines in mid-show. On the second day a man with fierce eyes appeared and I realised I had to be firm. Here's a snatch of the dialogue:
Fierce Eyes: Can I read?
Me: Yes.
Fierce Eyes: Right (walks away.)
(At this point I notice the bulgingness of his shoulder bag – and go after him.)
Me: (tactfully) You've got seven minutes.
Fierce Eyes: (glancing up from sorting his many bundles of A4 into one vast megabundle) My work cannot be cut. It must be heard as a whole or not at all.
Me: Not at all it is then. (I walk away.)
Seconds before the show starts:
Fierce Eyes: Seven minutes, then?
When his turn came he began:
'Due to the fascist organisation of this place I am only allowed to read for fifteen minutes. So I can let you hear only twenty of the seventy-seven sonnets I wrote during my last breakdown...'

But I do not want to give the wrong impression: The Lost Poets were not always quite so rigorously drilled and impeccably presented as I have suggested above. A tempering bohemianism was provided by Jim Hutcheson and his band which changed its name more frequently than its collars. 'What are you called today?' I remember asking him casually, as compere to performer, one day. 'The Great Deep', he improvised without hesitation. The show usually concluded with the company letting go with a few rousing choruses of Brian's 'With my Horns and my Wings and my Stabiliser Things' (a piece from his Early-Nihilist phase). This puzzled many, as we appeared to be miming or simply talking among ourselves – too bashful were we to sing loud enough and so overcome Jim's spirited accompaniment.

Our personnel changed only once when Jim Campbell, the editor of *New Edinburgh Review* (as this mighty organ you are reading was known in a previous life), took over from Liz after she went to Canada for a year.

A friend of ours, Cathlin McCaulay, made most money out of The Lost Poets: for £1 a day she agreed to sell the tickets at the door.

At the end of our three-week run she was £18 up – well ahead of the rest of us put together. 'The Lost Poets', a collection of our work slimly and limply vanitied to sell at reading under the stylish imprint 'Spineless Publications', was an attempt to recoup our finances. Maybe we should have tried T-shirts.

The ear is a much better critic than the eye. Through reading my work day after day, and listening to the others, I came to find my own voice and to be increasingly sensitive to what I wrote. Also, from well before The Lost Poets were 'founded' and right up to the present we have met to read each others' work and make helpful comments. Without this, I know I would never have written as I have. There was no Lost Poets' 'school' (perish the thought) as we all wrote quite differently. Andrew: hip, slick, with his philosophical and pop-music background; Brian: an anarchic humour that disclosed fundamental and disturbing truths; Liz: strongly into monologue, character and drama. And me still reading Shelley and marking out stresses. We wrote differently, stayed different, and have stayed good friends.

Some years ago we had a reunion dinner inspired by the unexpected discovery of a couple of bob plus interest still remaining in the lost Lost Poets post-office account book. Generously hosted by Brian and his partner Dilys Rose, the evening was given over to unashamed reminiscence as we passed around the publicity photograph. It ended with a heartfelt *tutti* of 'Horns and Wings...' A few laughs, a few tears and a good time was had by all.

I am surprised and delighted that so worthy a magazine as the *Edinburgh Review* should be concerned with The Lost Poets today; not many people were particularly interested in us even then.

Bibliography
Stretto (Outline Arts, 1976)
Creatures Tamed by Cruelty (EUSPB, 1979)
The Exquisite Instrument (Salamander Press, 1982)
The Tilting Room (Canongate, 1983)
Ragtime In Unfamiliar Bars (Secker & Warburg, 1985)
The Sound Of My Voice (Canongate, 1987; rpt. Paladin; revised edition Black Ace Books, 1994)
Histories of Desire (Bloodaxe, 1995)

from Night Visits: a novel

Ron Butlin

A FEW SECONDS before he died Malcolm's father raised his head from the pillow to look out at the falling snow. Loose flakes were being blown into the top corner of the window, flattening there until one by one they stuck to the glass. There was no sky anymore and no village; soon the garden itself would disappear.

Three months back he would have managed to the burn; then only to Robson's field; then the few yards to the start of the low road, with his stick testing the ground and Margaret helping. When he was a child the world had grown bigger every day, now it was shrinking on every side towards him at dead-centre.

He'd been dreaming about that small boat, the tiny metal yacht his father had made for him more than forty years ago. On the wall directly opposite there was a picture of swans flying over a stretch of river; he had dreamt being on the yacht and drifting easily downstream. By now he knew the landscape by heart: he could close his eyes again and hear the swans' wings beating loudly above him. Loud and steady for a moment, then more and more faint as they passed into the distance trailing silence after them.

He never saw them disappear, nor the trees, the line of low hills or the river itself. Only the small yacht remained, having come to rest in the palm of his hand for someone else to find later...

. . .

For the few weeks before his tenth birthday Malcolm saw the world only through his reflection's eyes.

One evening he'd been watching the first snowfall of the winter while click-click-clicking his fingers to the new chartbuster straight in at number seven. Usually at this time he would have been looking out the window for the builder's van that brought his dad home. Their meal in the oven to keep hot, he and his mum would have waited and, except for each flick as she turned over a page of her magazine, nothing would have happened. He'd have stared and stared into the darkness until finally the van came roaring up the hill, its lights sweeping the village cross where it braked to a stop just long enough for his dad to jump out, slamming the door behind. At once he'd have turned and rushed out of the kitchen to be at the gate to meet him. Now, with his dad ill in bed, everything in the house happened differently.

The snow was getting heavier. He couldn't see Stuart's Hill anymore; Robson's Farm had started drifting in and out of sight, swaying almost, as the snow around it held and fell with each sudden gust of wind.

'Close the curtains, please, Malcolm.'

Click-click-clicking his fingers louder he pretended not to hear.

'Dreaming, are you!' His mother laughed, then came across to the window, gave a quick tug and half the village was gone. In the next-door cottage with its porchlight a steadiness between the separate flakes, Sonny was probably playing with the new Gameboy he'd been given. Maybe his dad would recover in time to give *him* one for his birthday? Or maybe he could get his mum to drop a big hint the next time she was on the phone to Aunt Fiona, to save her buying him a book again or another jersey.

His mother had closed the other side, then straightened the curtains where they met. That was that, the night shut out: like giving up all hope until tomorrow that his dad would get any better.

'We'll be eating soon. Hands washed?'

He nodded. A double-finger click to hurry the record on, he wanted to sing along with the DJ's jingle if it ever came. Jingles were the best part: short and loud just like himself, his mother was always saying. She had started laying the table.

'Give's a hand, Malcolm, there's a good boy.'

He pulled open the top drawer of the sideboard where the forks and knives lay neatly, each piece in its correct compartment, with the napkins folded on one side.

'Your dad and all, mind.'

'Is he getting up?'

Even after being in his bed for weeks his dad still seemed to be getting older-looking and sweatier every day, and he coughed all the time. Above the sideboard was a large mirror that showed the room behind him with his mother putting the cups and plates silently on the table. If he could go into the mirror would it be completely silent, like when he dived into the swimming-pool? In there everything was exactly the same but when he leant closer, the glass was turned into soapwater colours or a rainbow along its edge; when he stepped back the colours became clear again. He stared straight into the eyes looking back at him: what would it feel like actually *being* his reflection? The same as looking into the room through a window maybe. He waved a fork, and his reflection was already waving it back. He laughed, stuck out his tongue.

'Come along, Malcolm, the tea's nearly ready. Doctor Marshall told your dad he should try getting up for his meals.'

He turned away from the mirror and in a sudden rush made two low-altitude bombing raids on the table: 'Forks away!' followed by 'Knives away!' Crouching to remain unseen by the enemy, he crept from cover to position the UN plane drops exactly on target: three places all set, the sauce-bottle and salt standing in the centre. Now for the moment he never liked: going into his dad's room 'I'll call him, will I?'

'You'll go in and tell him properly. If he's not up to it yet, say I'll bring him his dinner on a tray same as usual.'

He'd better hurry, the record was nearly ending and he didn't want to miss the jingle. Anyway, what was wrong with giving him a shout? He wasn't deaf, just ill. Having crossed the small lobby, he paused outside the door. Behind him, the record was swinging into the last chorus; he'd have to be quick. Because of the cold the window was never opened so his dad's room always stank of clothes-smell and bed-smell and illness-smell; a pity there was no letter-box to shout through.

He knocked, but not too loud in case his mother heard and would know he'd not gone in as he'd been told.

He waited, then bent down to the keyhole and whispered loudly:

'Dad, dad!' A faint light showed, so he must be awake. One last try at knocking, one last whisper:

'Dad!' But it was no good. He touched the doorhandle as lightly as possible, its metal surface felt greasy and disgusting, making him shiver all over. He turned it quickly and gave the door a push.

Half-open. The loud *tick-tick-tick* of the alarm clock; the sickly yellow of the bedlight; the heavy furniture that filled the rest of the room like darkness. And the smell getting worse by the second. It was like sticking his head underwater, and very dirty water at that.

Before going in he leant back into the corridor to take a deep breath, then pushed the door open wide:

'Dad, your tea's ready.'

His father was sitting up in bed looking directly at him as if he'd known he was going to enter the room exactly at that moment. His hands were rested on the covers and, as usual, he was wearing his pyjamas with a vest on underneath, the grey stained vest he never seemed to change. When he came through for tea he'd probably just put on a pullover and trousers on top.

The rest of his message delivered, Malcolm stood waiting. He repeated it:

'If you want, mum said she'd bring your dinner through. OK?'

Had his dad gone deaf suddenly? Or dumb? Well, he couldn't hold his breath any longer: a swallow of the underwater stink, then he went further into the room.

He reached out and tapped him lightly on the shoulder: 'Dad?'

He waited a moment, then nudged him harder.

All at once, without even turning to face him properly, his dad had begun sliding slowly towards him. Then falling.

He tried pushing him back: his dad was supposed to be ill, not playing games.

'Mum's waiting. We should go for tea, come on.'

Even though he was trying as hard as he could, he couldn't hold him from slipping further. Not his whole weight.

There was a loud *crack*: his father's head hitting full-force against the edge of the bedside table.

'Dad! Dad!'

Suddenly his mother was standing in the doorway; she was staring white-faced. She screamed. He pushed past her, rushed out of the room and a moment later was back in the kitchen where the Chartbuster Show was about to play the new number five and the table was laid for tea.

He heard her scream again.

The room was exactly the same as before but through the rasping tear in her voice he could feel his father's stubbled cheek still scraping his own, and the boniness of his jaw.

Quickly, before another scream came, he covered his ears. He was standing rigidly still in the centre of the room, facing the silence of the sideboard mirror where there was no screaming, no weight pressing on top of him nor the terrible *crack* his father's head had made as he fell. In the mirror everything was ready for them to sit down and eat tea as usual.

He went up to the sideboard and looked closer.

Taking his hands away from his ears, he reached towards the glass where his reflection's hands were already reaching towards his. Their fingertips touched. After a moment's hesitation he pressed harder breaking through into the silence underneath.

His reflection and himself together, looking out for the first time. As though seeing the room through his reflection's eyes:

Everything in the kitchen happening as it should do: the plates laid out, the chairs in position, the two-bar fire, and you standing by yourself in front of the mirror. You can still hear your mother's screams but as they are on the *outside* now, they can no longer hurt you. You should take your seat at the table and wait for her return.

...

What had she done wrong?

If she was holding the bible she would be safe.

Her slightest movement rubbed her body against her night dress, against the sheet. Temptation.

Temptation, and then sin. Wickedness.

She'd almost run out of the old woman's room, as if trying to get further and further from the flames of hell she'd felt touch her.

What had she done wrong?

Over the years she had pared her life down to the most basic elements to keep herself safe. Apart from her church-commitments she never went out in the evening, never had visitors. She'd created a pattern for her life, a routine that protected her. At forty-seven years old she had thought herself beyond danger.

Like always she'd been settled in her armchair by the fire, the door closed, curtains pulled, the reading lamp on. She'd been up since seven and had hardly stopped once all day, what with the paperwork, the staff, and over two hours wasted at the Lothian Health Board offices. She didn't ask for much: to be left to arrange her evenings in her own way; to close the door, pull the curtains, get settled by the fire bothering no-one and no-one bothering her. She'd phoned Margaret in the afternoon to ask if her husband was showing any improvement – did that not count for something? Once she was certain Stella was through in the staffroom watching TV, and the residents in their rooms, she had relaxed. With God's Word for company there should have been nothing to do but keep her eyes open and keep turning the pages. She should have been safe and secure.

She knew the words by heart and had repeated them aloud whenever her attention wandered. That had always worked before. The rest of the room was in half-shadow; all that mattered was the lamplight and her bible. Had the sound of rain begun she wouldn't even have listened for the patterns it made against the glass; she didn't do that any more. Bed at ten-thirty, and the night-hours reduced to a certainty the shape and size of the sleeping-pill she would swallow and be finished with in a moment. That's what should have happened.

From now on she'd take her pills even earlier if need be. Then, she could snap her fingers at the rain, the flames could burn her and she would simply turn over and sleep.

Had it been her sister's phone-call? Until then everything had gone just as it should: she'd been reading from the Book of Ruth, whispering a few of the verses aloud every so often to keep herself on course for bed. Her voice was company; it returned her to where she was: sitting beside her own fire, in her own house. That's when the phone rang – if only it had been some relative wanting to visit one of the residents tomorrow, or a new resident maybe. She'd answered it in her professional voice:

'Rosehaven Nursing Home. Fiona McBride speaking.'

The instant she realised it was Margaret and why she was calling she'd changed to a more personal tone. All in all the conversation had been handled very well. She'd been sympathetic; with her experience she'd known exactly the right questions to ask, and could make the proper responses when required. She'd been patient, too, while her sister repeated and repeated that Peter had been on the mend; that he'd been expected to get up for tea; that the doctor had told her the worst was past; that it was Malcolm who had found him. Then the tears. Then the same story all over again from the start. She'd been a good listener though, and by the end had managed to bring her some comfort. Offering to go down for the funeral was one thing, but she shouldn't have suggested they come to stay. It had been a kind thought, of course, but having her sister in the house, having Malcolm especially, would upset her routine. Her routine was all she had.

Only after she'd calmed herself by listening to the even *tick-tick* of the mantelpiece clock had she been able to continue reading. She had never succeeded in making an interesting pattern out of its predictably steady stroke. Unlike rain, for then the wind could always alter its force against the glass to change its sound and sometimes even silence it for several beats at a time. A few more pages and it would have been time to put away her bible, take her pill, have a last word with Stella before going up to her room. Then the temptation began:

The upstairs corridor with a table lamp at each landing, and the line of closed doors. Closed doors with their spy-holes for looking in. Closed doors that could open.

She had her routine, and she would stick to it: she'd pressed herself deeper into her chair. Two pills, she decided, maybe even three after hearing her sister's sad news.

Pausing outside one of the rooms, turning the handle. The sound of someone breathing.

She'd tried to keep reading, she'd really tried: 'And an angel of the Lord came up from Gilgal.'

Darkness apart from a faint nightlight shining on the bedside table.

'And an angel of the Lord came up from Gilgal.'

Then she began reading aloud: 'And an angel of the Lord came

up from Gilgal to Bochim.'
The bedroom would be warm. She would have to move cautiously and make no noise.
'Came up from Gilgal to Bochim and said, I made you to go up out of Israel –'
Being careful not to waken the sleeper.
'Made you go up out of Israel –'
The stillness in the room, the half-darkness, the smell of old age.
'To-go-up-out-of-Israel –'
She'd watched herself put the book aside, switch off the gas fire, and go into the hall. She paused, listened. The only sound was from Stella's TV at the back of the house. She began climbing the stairs. The first floor. Breathing quicker already, smiling to herself. Everything was under control. This was an adventure, a harmless walk along the upstairs corridor at night. Mrs Collins's door: a quick glance through the spy-hole to check the old dear was comfortable. Having a quick glance, that was all she was doing. Nothing more. Quite under control.

But now she'd seen into one of the rooms, seen the ornaments and photographs, the head on the pillow. She should have gone to bed, but she couldn't. She felt more excited, she just *had* to go into one of the rooms and touch the ornaments, examine the photographs. What had she thought she was doing?

A glance into the next room and into the next after that, breathing quicker each time. What had she thought she was looking for? Up to the second floor: every step taken so carefully and silently along the corridor. Mrs Southwick's door; Mr Blackwood's; Mrs Tait's.

At the top stair of the third-floor landing she'd almost slipped. She rested there for a moment, held the banisters to steady herself. That was to be her last chance to go back, to take her pill, two pills, three, however many she had to, and go safely to her room and to sleep. But then she would have had to let go the banisters, unclasp her fingers, turn and force herself back every step of the way to her room downstairs. She should have known what was right, and what was temptation. Standing at the top of the stairs, hesitating whether or not to go further along the corridor and into one of the rooms: that hesitation should have been enough to have told her; that sense of longing, of expectation and excitement – of desire.

The hall clock chimed the hour. She had clung to the sound of each separate chime to keep herself where she was and not go forward. Eight – nine – ten –

Silence.

Only the polished wood to grasp onto, curving upwards under her palm, arching her fingers, pushing her forwards almost, towards the darkened corridor, towards the closed doors. This floor was the worst: the bedridden, the sick and simple. Her hands were shaking, sweat was trickling down her back. There were six doors: three on either side. Mrs Davidson, Mrs Connaught, Mrs Byrd, Mr Wells, Mrs Goldfire. The last room was unoccupied. Rather than go in there with its bed stripped, its dressing-table cleared of ornaments, she would have started her search all over again. Was that where all temptation led: to be trapped forever in one moment of the night, rushing from floor to floor, room to room?

She took a deep breath, then tried each door in turn. Pausing long enough until she was certain: Mrs Davidson's, Mrs Connaught's, Mrs Byrd's. Leaning against the door frames to rest, but she had to keep going. Outside Mrs Goldfire's. Yes, the same panelled wood, the same paintwork: and yet feeling so different from the others. As if she recognised it. She had to go in. The certainty of its being the right room had been such relief that she was almost shaking as she began turning the handle.

Having closed the door soundlessly behind her, she stood for a moment perfectly still, then switched on the bedlight. Mrs Goldfire was lying on her back with her bedcap half on the pillow, half on her nearly bald scalp, while she breathed lightly but steadily; her right hand was out of the covers.

For that last second it had seemed as if she were watching herself standing in the old woman's room; as if all her life until then she had been merely the observer of another's longing; and suddenly there was no *other*. Had she, in dreams perhaps, rehearsed to perfection what she was about to do? She moved with a sureness that thrilled her. Firstly, the photographs: a wedding in black and white, a group of children, a bungalow with a couple and a dog outside. She glanced at them one by one, running her fingers over the glass and metal frames, tracing out someone's features, a prominent forehead, a smile. Then she laid them face down. From behind her came the sound of the old woman's thin strengthless breathing. In the dressing-table mirror the bedlight showed one side of Mrs Goldfire's face lined and mottled, the other in shadow. Next came the ornaments: a small china cat; a dark wooden box containing a few earrings, a cheap-looking bracelet and a necklace; a fan spread open to reveal a Spanish dancer with 'A Present from Seville' printed on the plastic handle. She picked it up, snapped it shut, opened it and fanned herself while she took a few steps up and down the space between the bed and the chest of drawers. The charm bracelet had a broken clasp; she weighted the heavy necklace in her hand but felt, even then, it was the wrong colour. Luckily there were a few scent-bottles: she unscrewed each top in turn and had a smell – old women's perfumes. The eau-de-Cologne almost made her dizzy with excitement. She breathed it in, closed her eyes briefly, and there, without any effort on her part, was her mother's bedroom once more; with its curtains open to show that bright September morning over ten years ago.

Another deep breath and she could make out the figure lying with its head on the pillow, its hand stretched out towards her. She sighed, smiled to herself, then replaced the stopper and put the small glass bottle in exactly the same spot it had been before. Two steps, three and she was holding the covers, the stitched hem of the sheet. She must get onto her knees; she must press her face into the smell of the blankets, no longer disgusting as it had been all those years ago, but sweet. Intoxicating. She fumbled for the old lady's hand. She knew exactly what she had to say:

'I'm sorry I didn't come sooner. Really sorry.' Whispering while she caressed the old woman's open palm. 'I wanted to, you must understand. More than anything I wanted to come to you. But I wasn't sure.' She squeezed each finger in turn, very gently.

The old lady's hand was resting lightly on her head. Yes, that was what she had come for. That was how it should have been all those years ago: the smell of the bedclothes, the frailty of the hand, the slow breathing, and the closeness between them – that, most of all. The bony fingers lay unsteadily on her hair, then caressed her face. Nothing else mattered, only the touch of that hand on her cheek smoothing the hair away from her eyes, tracing out the shape of her mouth. Nothing else mattered except the tenderness. The love.

There was a moment of such utter peace she had almost wept with gratitude to be there; surely that was true forgiveness. Then the moment passed.

She felt her mouth going dry; her tongue sliding against her teeth. She swallowed, then gripped the old woman's hand tighter. That was when her nipples began hardening, her thighs began aching to be touched: she turned and almost ran from the room, her whole body burning, burning. Wickedness, wickedness, wickedness.

She could see the ceiling curved above her by her tears.

Ron Butlin was born in Edinburgh in 1949, and studied at the University of Edinburgh. Since 1979 he has been a full-time writer. Besides his radio plays, much of his work has been broadcast in Britain and abroad, and his poetry and fiction have been translated into over ten languages. He has been a Writer in Residence at the Universities of Edinburgh, Stirling, and New Brunswick, Canada. At present he is completing his third novel. He lives in Edinburgh with his wife and their dog.

THE TABOO-WORD TOTEM

DUNCAN McLEAN

WILLY MALEY

DAVID STENHOUSE

CHRISTOPHER WHYTE

ALAN FREEMAN

IAN CADMAN

(i) Obscene, ie. matter tending to deprave and corrupt those whose minds are open to such immoral influences, and into whose hands the matter is likely to fall... An instance of action by the government to restain the sale of printed matter on the score of alleged obscenity is afforded by the well-known case of Joyce's *Ulysses*. An edition of 500 numbered copies, published by John Rodker, Paris for the Egoist Press, London, in January 1923, was confiscated (with it is said the exception of one copy) by the British Customs Authorities... *Lady Chatterley's Lover* by D. H. Lawrence was the subject of the case *Regina v. Penguin Books Limited*, heard at the Old Bailey in 1960 (20 Oct.-2 Nov.). The case, which resulted in the acquittal of Penguin Books and the release of the book for sale, was interesting because for the first time the defendants were allowed to bring witnesses to give evidence on the literary and moral qualities of the book. In 1964 an amending act, aimed at the traffic in and display of pornography, created a new offence of '*having* an obscene article for publication for gain', a clause which was applied in 1967 to the conviction of a bookseller for stocking H. Selby Jnr's *Last Exit to Brooklyn*. This decision was reversed on appeal in 1968, and in 1976 the 'not guilty' verdict on a paperback called *Inside Linda Lovelace* convinced prosecuting authorities that the pursuit of written works with slightest pretension to serious purpose would be counter-productive.

The Oxford Companion to English Literature, 1985

Unable to discriminate clearly between words and things, the savage commonly fancies that the link between a name and the person or thing denominated by it is not a mere arbitrary and ideal association, but a real and substantial bond which unites the two in such a way that magic may be wrought on a man just as easily through his name as through his hair, his nails, or any other material part of his person.

'Tabooed Words', J. G. Frazer, *The Golden Bough*, 1922

Taboo is a Polynesian word, the translation of which provides difficulties for us because we no longer possess the idea which it connotes. It was still current with the ancient Romans: their word 'sacer' was the same as the taboo of the Polynesians...

... For us the meaning of taboo branches off into two opposite directions. On the one hand it means to us sacred, consecrated: but on the other hand it means uncanny, dangerous, forbidden, and unclean. The opposite for taboo is designated in Polynesian by the word *nos* and signifies something ordinary and generally accessible. Thus something like the concept of reserve inheres in taboo; taboo expresses itself essentially in prohibitions and restrictions. Our combination of 'holy dread' would often express the meaning of taboo.

Totem and Taboo, Sigmund Freud, 1919

Censorship is, and always has been, throughout history, a tool of authority to withhold authority from other people, to attain authority for itself. It is a means of control. It is a means of oppression. It is a way of stopping other people from becoming educated enough, and intelligent enough, to think for themselves and to share in that authority, or to become themselves authoritative. It is an anti-democratic weapon and if any country pretends to be democratic there should be no place for censorship.

This certainly applies to Great Britain. I do not like everything that is published. Nevertheless I would not stop anything from being published because the only possible protection that we can have in society from something that we all recognise to be bad, to be nasty, to be in its way evil, is to allow complete freedom of expression, so that anybody can publish an exposure. We must hope that if our reasoning is sound it will prevail.

John Calder, *The Arts in a Permissive Society*, London 1971

> Common speech, as we know, is full of erotic metaphors which are applied to matters that have nothing to do with sex; and conversely, sexual symbolism by no means implies that the interests making use of it are by nature erotic.
>
> C. G. Jung, *Symbols of Transformation*, New York 1943

> About fifteen years ago you had this stupid carry on where you weren't allowed to use 'fuck' unless you were talking about the act of screwing, you know. Now, it was never ever used, I never heard it used that way in my life until I started hearing Kenneth Tynan talking on television about D. H. Lawrence. I'd never heard that. In my experience no one ever used the work 'fuck' in that way.
>
> from *James Kelman Interviewed*,
> in Edinburgh Review 71, republished 1995 in
> *Nothing is Altogether Trivial*, ed. Murdo Macdonald

> FUCK. v.t. and i. To have sexual connexion (with): v.i. of either sex, v.t. only of the male : a vulgar., C.16-20. The earliest and latest dictionaries to record it are Florio [1598] (s.v. *fottere*) and Grose [1785], the O.E.D., S.O.D., E.D.D. all 'banning' it (cf. note at c**t): the efforts of James Joyce and D. H. Lawrence have not restored it to its orig. dignified status. Either ex- Gr. φυτεύω, L. *futuere*, Fr. *foutre*, the medial c. and the abridged form being due to a Teutonic radical and A.S. tendency, or more prob., as A. W. Read (after Kluge) convincingly maintains, ex Ger. *ficken*, lit. to strike, hence to copulate with: cf., therefore, *bang* and *knock*.
>
> *A Dictionary of Slang and Unconventional English*,
> Eric Partridge, London 1937

An ABC of Bad Language

Duncan McLean

A is for Aye
Early in 1994 a man was found to be in contempt of court by a judge in Glasgow, and fined. His crime was answering a question with the word Aye. The judge knew what the word meant, everyone in the court knew what it meant, but still the judge felt it necessary to refuse the man's right to use the word. The judge insisted that the word to be used was Yes. The man couldn't see why he should be forced to use somebody else's vocabulary, when his own was adequate to the situation. The judge understood, however, that folk speaking in their own voice is the first step down a road that leads to them thinking their own thoughts and taking control of their own lives. The state doesn't want people being in control of their own lives, so when opportunities arise it will force people into adopting a voice of which it approves, or into silence. Maybe the clearest day to day examples of this can be found in the education system and in the media. It was good of the judge to remind us that the legal system is just as committed to free speech: We're free to speak what They allow.

B is for By-The-Glass
On his way back from exile to join in the revolution in 1917, Lenin paused at the small town of Razliv. Here he pondered and planned his intervention in the uprising, an episode later immortalised in various gospelized versions of his life. and in a famous painting by Soviet artist A. A. Rylov, *Lenin v Razlivye*. Unfortunately, as well as meaning 'Lenin in Razliv', that phrase also means 'Lenin By-The-Glass', from the verb *razlivat*, to pour out. During the Brezhnev era, a flood of jokes employing this pun started to circulate, eg. that an official Soviet vodka was to be introduced named *Lenin v Razlivye*. Obviously, the Kremlin could not tolerate this disrespect. They acted decisively, officially changing the spelling and pronunciation of the verb for pouring to *rozlivat*, making the subversion of the system by pun impossible.

C is for Cunt

Recently I was asked to write a short story for *The Big Issue in Scotland*. I came up with one called 'Below Zero/Them Thar Hills'. When it was published, I was surprised to see various changes had been made without consulting me. The title was different, for one thing. Another was that the words cunt and fucking had been replaced by c*** and f******. It seems that *The Big Issue* had been worried about offending readers. Quite right! What's the point in upsetting folk who're supporting your good cause? Why stop with cunt and fucking, though? Words like poverty and homelessness are surely far more offensive – the conditions they describe certainly are – so here's hoping that in future *The Big Issue* and other publications will protect our sensibilities further by referring always to p****** and h************.

Duncan McLean's latest novel *B*****M*** is reviewed elsewhere in this issue.

The original syllable or root-word for the vulva in the Mediterranean world was *cu* or *cwe*. The Egyptian word *ka-t* was used both for the female sex organs, including the vagina, and the mother. The Sanskrit word is *yoni*, but the alternative word *kunti* was also used in contexts signifying the female principle or the wife of a deity. The name is related to Cynnthus (Kunthus), Greek goddess of fecundity.

The Greek words are *kteis* and *konnos*. The Latin equivalents include: *cunnus* (from the Greek), *concha* (conch), *navis* (boat), *porca* (sow), *pudenda muliebris* (sex parts of the female), *sinus* (cavity), *sulcus* (furrow), *tubus* (tube), *vesica* (bladder). Other terms are *kvithe* (Teutonic), *qitbus* (Gothic), *cwithe* (Old English, also meaning 'womb'), *cunte* or *counte* (Old Middle English), *queynte* (in Chaucer's Miller's Tale).

Encyclopedia of Esoteric Man, ed. Walker, London 1977

Swearing Blind: Kelman and the Curse of the Working Classes

Willy Maley

> You taught me language, and my profit on't
> Is, I know how to curse. The red plague rid you
> For learning me your language!
> (Shakespeare, *The Tempest*, I.ii.362-64)

> A little onward lend thy guiding hand
> To these dark steps, a little furder on.
> (Milton, *Samson Agonistes*, 1-2)

James Kelman is no Caliban, but, like Prospero's, his creations know how to curse. Sammy Samuels gropes his way through *How Late It Was, How Late*, effing and blinding as he goes. Sammy, a latter-day Samson, eyeless in Glasgow, is deprived of his sight, like so many critics when confronted with Kelman. They hear only the tap, tap, tap of what they perceive as 'bad' language, which they speak of in blankety-blanket terms. Let's remove the clothespins of quotation marks, including the one for the nose, and call a spade a fucking shovel. Kelman writes in the name of fuck. Where in the name of fuck? On the very first page of *How Late It Was, How Late*. There it is: 'Where in the name of fuck …' (p. 1) There are those who would see in Kelman's work an inclination towards swearing for its own sake, for fuck's sake. The second paragraph of his latest novel finds the main character sporting 'an auld pair of trainer shoes for fuck sake'.

Kelman not only swears like fuck, in the name of fuck, and for fuck's sake, but he *can* swear like fuck. It's a question not just of frequency, or inclination, but of ability, range and intensity. On the whole, when it comes to swearing, Kelman is unbeatable. In the field of creative cursing there is nobody who can touch him. But this, too, is to miss the point. Kelman is not just good at 'bad' language, he is good with language, full stop. There is nothing good or bad but thinking makes it so, and in Kelman's case any attempt to separate out the so-called bad language, the swearing and cursing, either for praise or blame, is already an act of blindness rather than insight.

Yet Kelman's writing has become synonymous with swearing. If the issue is 'bad language', supposing that such a thing exists, then Kelman is your man. His language is 'bad' in the American sense. It has attitude. Bad here means good, loud and proud, like a ghettoblaster packed with big audio dynamite. Kelman's language is explosive. He is effusive, efficacious. In fact, Kelman knows 'fuck all'. That is, he knows all there is to know about 'fuck'. In Kelman's writing, 'fuck' functions as a transcendental signifier. For fuck's sake is for God's sake. He uses eff in mysterious ways. 'Fuck' covers a multitude of syntax, doing service as modifier, intensifier, adjective, noun, and verb. The use of what linguists call 'fucking-insertion' is exemplary. For example, 'neverfuckingending' (p. 39), or better still 'enerfuckinggetic, enerfuckinggenetised' (p. 174), or what about 'dysfuckingfunctional'. (p. 248) Kelfuckingman, know what I'm talking about? JamesbastardingKelman. Kelman is abusive, not insofar as he abuses language, or uses abusive language. Disabuse yourself of that idea at once. No, Kelman is abusive in terms of his grip on the language of abuse. He swears it well. But, like Joyce's left hand, he does a lot of other things besides, and there's the rub. To be or effen bee, that is the question.

Sammy tells a would-be legal representative: 'There's a difference between repping somebody and fucking being somebody'. (p. 241) It is a difference that philosophers and literary critics have struggled with for centuries. Kelman is not Sammy. He'll never be him, no matter how much effing and beeing he employs to represent him with truth, honesty and integrity. Helen, Sammy's partner, 'didnay think the same as her man she thought like the guy that was fucking repping him, know what I'm saying, that was the crack, she thought the same way as Sammy's rep but no like Sammy, like him himself'. (p. 321) Him himself. Himself alone. Solitary Sammy, a singular self up against the state. Represented by Kelman, of course, both the self and the state, as if the self wasn't the state's smartest invention, and its most prized secret weapon. With Kelman, expletives are not deleted, or under erasure. Representation has given way to being, or effing and beeing, to be more precise.

Sammy's self-loathing goes hand-in-hand with his self-determination: 'It was all down to Sammy; every fucking last fucking thing man know what I mean know what I fucking mean it was down to him, Sammy, Sammy himself man that was who it was down to, him, nay other cunt, all this fucking crap man it was his and nay other cunt's, fucking his'. (p. 322-23) Or again: 'He was a blind bastard. Right then. That stage ye just go, Fuck it, cause what else is there? nothing, there's fuck all'. (p. 324) This is possessive individualism, bourgeois individualism, taken to its extreme. It's a sort of blindness, too. Blind to history and politics and philosophy. But this is Sammy's blindness. It is not necessarily Kelman's. Macdonald Daly's diatribe against what he rechristened *A Disinfectant* made the mistake of conflating author and character, Kelman and Patrick Doyle.[1] It is tempting, all too tempting, to see in Sammy Samuels Kelman 'himself': 'Nay other cunt; no the fucking sodjers man, no fucking naybody, just him, him himself'. (p. 326) The same system that produces the 'sodjers' also creates the dissident selves who oppose it. Sammy has his moments of insight, like the alcoholic's fleeting periods of clarity, when he sees that his tormentors 'werenay fucking god almighty they were just fucking people, that's all they were, people, ordinary people; bampot bastards, but people'. (pp. 333-34) This is much more palatable than a demonology that satanises the state and sanitises the self.

The question of being and representation – aesthetic and political – is raised rather than resolved in Kelman's work. Kelman reps and raps, he effs and bees. To be or not to be, but instead to represent, that is the fucking question. It is a question, above all, of nation, class, and gender. Swearing is the phatic communion of the factory, the barracks, the pub, the street. A sign of violent and impoverished masculinity, disenfranchised youth, socialised labour. 'Fuck' is both taboo and totem, it is both unspeakable and unduly fetishized. The focus on context has to include the nation. As well as a class context, and an urban context, there is a national context. Like Hamlet, we must 'speak of country matters', because swearing and national identity are intimately bound up together. The Booker controversy saw critics line up to defend or denounce Kelman on the strength of his language, and it was often stated that swearing was a special property of Scots, of Kelman's national language, or local dialect.

There are those readers who try to outKelman Kelman. Sworn enemies of Kelman think that by out-swearing him they have answered his call, his challenge, as though it all came down to a swearing contest. This is the kind of macho posturing, the intellectual equivalent of armwrestling, that we get from Macdonald Daly. The more-working-class-than-thou attitude. You can get a good price on the open market for working-class credibility these days. I've floated my own company there at times, and never been bought out yet. Daly's vitriolic parody in *Cencrastus* seems to me to say little beyond 'Look at me. I can swear too'. As though Kelman's literary genius could be reduced to cursing. Some of these critics have 'pen envy', and this expresses itself in a desire to dismiss Kelman in a cursory fashion as a talking swear-box. Those who can, do. Those who can't, fuck. Whether censoring or competing, whether celebrating or carping, the critics who concentrate on so-called 'bad' or 'strong' language get nowhere, or, if there is a destination, then they get to 'fuck'. That is as far as they get.

Those who can't swear or won't swear, in other words those who don't give a fuck, are a different matter. They might like to imagine a cursefree Kelman, one that would lose the shell of bad language but retain the kernel of good storytelling. This is another blind alley. The swearing is integral to Kelman's power as a writer. It is neither a vulgar and superfluous supplement nor an offensive coating concealing shortcomings in narrative, dialogue, or characterisation. To focus on the swearing to the exclusion of all else is to lose one's eyesight, to be blind to the text. I'm thinking here of Ron McKay's recurrent criticisms of Kelman in *Scotland on Sunday*, enumerating the fucks in Kelman's work. Neal Ascherson rightly ridiculed the kind of myopic individual who would invest time in counting curses in order to announce that there are 4,000 fucks in *How Late It Was, How Late*. Fuck-counting could overtake trainspotting as the pastime of the anorak brigade. There are none so blind as those who will not swear, or those who see only swear-words, like red neon signs flashing stop, or the bleeps that tell blind people when to cross.

Anyway, what is bad, strong, abusive, offensive, vulgar about any language? The doctor who examines Sammy tells him: 'I find your language offensive', but reading their exchange, the reader – this reader at least – is struck most forcibly by the offensiveness of the doctor's language. (p. 225) The chauvinistic responses to Kelman, social and national, can with more justification be labelled 'bad'. Sammy says: 'Funny how ye tell people a story to make a point and ye fail, ye fail, a total disaster'. (p. 17) Kelman fails only if we focus on the fucks, man, just the fucks. That's not the whole story. It's not even half the story, but. That 'but' at the end of a sentence is more indicative of Kelman's style than a hundred well-placed fucks.

There are those readers who might say of Kelman: 'Nice lexis, shame about the fucks', as though the proliferation of swear-words somehow detracts from the rich urban Glaswegian dialect. Kelman is allegedly to blame for the focus on the swearing. It's his fault. As Sammy says, 'Ye do yer crime ye take yer time'. But few critics who dwell on the 'bad' language take their time. The very idea of 'bad language' is of course linked to a particular elitist theory of art. This theory of art, as Kelman has pointed out a hundred times, constructs a hierarchy of discourses and values some ways of speaking above others. Kelman's use of Scots is tightly meshed with his use of swearing, and this allows his detractors to fasten upon the latter when their chief objection is to the former. As the OED defines it, fuck is 'vulgar', and vulgar means 'used only by those who have no wish to be thought either polite or educated'. If 'fuck' is vulgar, then 'cunt' is both vulgar, when applied to 'female genitals', and 'derogatory', when used to describe an 'unpleasant or stupid person', like the one who devised this limited entry. So much for the fucking OED.

How Late It Was, How Late is itself a marvellous blend of blindness and insight. In the land of the blind Sammy Samuels is a visionary: 'Now here he was blind, 'fucking blind'. Imagine going blind. Christ. What a turn-up for the books that was'. (p. 23) And of course we can only imagine it if we are sighted. Kelman can only imagine it. When one sense goes others become finely tuned. Touch, taste, smell, and of course, hearing. As Sammy reminds us: 'He was fucking blind man he wasnay deaf'. (p. 41) It's all in the voice, in what is audible. To be heard but not seen, that is the curse of the working class. In life, in literature, in politics.

The moving cursor writes, and having cursed moves on. Kelman is cursive and discursive, but the curses come home to roost. Swearing is the curse of Kelman, insofar as it acts as a magnet, a focal point, or a fuck-all point, where all critics cross and confer and conspire against the big picture. Kelman's fiction struggles under a curse, *the curse*, perhaps, the bloody curse or the curse of blood, a corpuscular condition. Sammy is a great believer in 'some physical activity to help out the brainbox, it paces ye, keeps the corpuscles circulating Sammy it gets the blood pumping, the auld oxygen'. (p. 304) Sammy is 'bloody blind', but 'It wasnay his fault he was fucking blind!' (p. 46) For Sammy, there is no asylum, only escape. The 'Blind Asylum' conjures up visions of 'some fucking victorian nightmare' (p. 67). Blinded by the 'state authorities', Sammy discovers that being blind means being at the mercy of those authorities in the most acute way.

There are no swear-words in the title, on the dustjacket, or in the flyleaf, but the swearing is not ob-scene, offstage. It is not reduced to noises off. There is no overarching narrative voice that minds its P's and Q's. This is an advance on the traditional separation between swearing and speaking on the one hand and a polite third person voice on the other. Here the hands are rubbing together.

Erstwhile etymologists will be aware of the fact that 'swear' and 'answer' derive from the same root, from the Germanic word 'swarjan'. Kelman has all the answers. He is an answering-machine. Leave a fucking message and he'll get back to you.

Kelman's swearing has for a time excluded him from schools, from temples of learning. To be 'profane' is to be *pro fanus*, before, or outside *fanus*, the temple, to be forsworn, to be cursed. The shift in education policy in favour of allowing Kelman – and other authors – to be studied in schools, and the general opening up of the curriculum to contemporary fiction, is a positive sign. For Kelman's are not porridge oaths, couthy kailyard curses from the cabbage patch. There's no 'Jings, crivvens, help ma boab!' for Kelman. Nor was he stung by Matt McGinn's Effen Bee.

Swearing is like snoring. You're always the last to know. It must be bound up in some way with the subconscious, with blind spots and lacunae in language. Like the woman from my native Possil who boldly declared: 'No cunt swears up this close', or the mother who told her child to 'stop that fucking swearing!' Kelman swears like a trooper, or rather Sammy does, if we draw the distinction between being and representing upon which Sammy insists so vehemently, and which one suspects Kelman endorses.

The Scottish socialist historian, James Young, expresses the view of one who has had to rethink his position on swearing:

> ... in the early 1970s I already began to question the orthodox socialist attitude towards swearing and swear-words as Kelman is now raising. In the 1950s and 60s I had been impressed by the counter-objections of Jean Jaures and Leon Trotsky. Before I began to do serious work on labour history in the late 1960s, I had been impressed by Trotsky's argument that: 'Abusive language and swearing are a legacy of slavery, humiliation, and disrespect for human dignity – one's own and that of other people.' The really interesting and typical thing was that Trotsky wanted to use authoritarian means to create human dignity. Therefore he approved of the decision taken inside a Russian factory after the Revolution to 'solve' the problem by imposing fines on those who used swear-words.[2]

Few academics swear in print. One exception is the black American feminist bell hooks, Distinguished Professor of English at the City University in New York. She describes her language as: 'Polyphonic, it combines the many voices I speak – academic talk, standard English, vernacular patois, the language of the street'.[3] Kelman too – despite the charges of incomprehensibility or monotony by the Rabbi Julia Neuberger, or any new bugger who takes exception to his tone and tongue – is polyphonic.

As well as asserting copyright, the preliminary matter of the novel informs the reader that: 'The author has asserted his moral rights'. This ought to surprise no-one. Kelman is an intensely moral author, and his is a moral tale, a story of the triumph of the individual spirit over 'the state authorities', to use the language of the dustjacket. The fact that this individual is an historical product of these self-same 'state authorities', and of a chauvinist, ethnocentric and masculine Western ideology, need not trouble us here, as it seems not to trouble Kelman. Personally, I find the lack of any appeal to social or communal responses to injustice in contemporary Scottish fiction depressing. The opposition between a state that is caricatured and ridiculed and an individual who is sanctified and championed is, for me, sterile and fruitless.

Did I say there was no such thing as 'bad language'? Yes, I believe I did. Does Kelman think so too? I'm not so sure. There is always a tension between the right to free speech and the principle of no platform for racism, sexism, and other forms of discriminatory discourse. The utopian idea of literature as a space within which one can in principle say anything is compromised by demands for political correctness and social justice. Sammy advises his son to avoid the word 'darkies': 'Right; aye well ... the thing is, ye shouldnay call people names; that's the thing, ye have to watch that ... Sammy sniffed. Know what I'm saying son it's a thing to watch for [...] All I'm saying son if people don't want ye to call them a name, ye shouldnay call them it; just one of these things.' (p. 345) There are feminists – and others – who would count the word 'cunt' among those names that one shouldn't be called. It's a question of being and representation, and it's political through and through. There's no literary get-out clause, no contract that absolves an author of responsibility, duty, and obligation to the other.

Kelman's best friend is his derogative. The cur is not a curse but a four-lettered friend. It answers to the name of 'Fuck', not Fido. It answers in the name of 'fuck'. 'Fuck', according to the dictionary definition, is a bit of a bastard, a mongrel, perhaps. Its origins are unknown. Its roots lie in the sixteenth-century, but it has branches everywhere. Even the dedication contains an oath: 'Alasdair Gray, Tom Leonard, Agnes Owens and Jeff Torrington are still around, thank christ'. So too is Kelman, and for a long time yet, one hopes. Thank fuck. Neal Ascherson, commenting on the headline in *The Independent* that blared: '"Foul-mouthed" novel is a £20,000 Booker winner', insists that 'Kelman has his own window in the house of languages'.[4] I would argue that Kelman has a houseful of windows, and that the smashed pane of so-called bad language represents the boarded-up blindness of a blank critical gaze.

Ironically, the blinding itself is glossed over. Sammy's beating at the hands of the 'state authorities' is curtailed with these words: 'But ye're as well drawing a curtain here, nay point prolonging the agony'. (p. 6) There are other blanks. The 'political' crimes that the police are interested in are never fully elaborated. They serve, though, to create the impression that there is a political sphere outside of Sammy's predicament, something that the novel itself works to undermine. Sammy doesn't like having 'blank-outs'. (p. 170) He had one just before being blinded. The 'state authorities' don't like these blanks either. Anything could happen in the space of a blank. Perhaps that's what troubles people so much about Kelman's language, it's not just the beings, but the fucking in-betweens. 'I swear too much dont I!', Sammy declares shortly before his departure. As if to atone, the final page is swear-free, a veritable fucking blind spot, as Sammy disappears 'out of sight'.

References

1. Macdonald Daly, 'Your Average Working Kelman', *Cencrastus* (Autumn, 1993), pp. 14-16.
2. James D. Young, 'Scotland at the Crossroads: An Introduction', in James D. Young (ed.), *Scotland at the Crossroads: A Socialist Answer* (Clydeside Press: Glasgow, 1990), p. 22, citing Leon Trotsky, *Problems of Everyday Life* (New York, 1973), p. 52.
3. bell hooks, *Outlaw Culture: Resisting Representations* (London: Routledge, 1994), p. 7.
4. Neal Ascherson, 'Will Kelman's London cheers pave the way for Glasgow sneers?', *Independent On Sunday* (16 October, 1994).

Willy Maley lectures in English Literature at the University of Glasgow. He is also a playwright, with eight performed works to his name, the three most recent staged by the award-winning CAT. A Theatre Company.

A would-be Führer, full of enthusiasm for the dictatorship of the proletariat, was also enthusiastic about sex-economy. He came to me and said: 'You are wonderful. Karl Marx has shown the people how they can be free *economically*. You have shown the people how they can be free *sexually*: you have told them "Go out and fuck as much as you like."' In your head everything becomes a perversion. What I call the loving embrace becomes, in your life, a pornographic act.
Listen, Little Man!, Wilhelm Reich, New York 1948

A Wholly Healthy Scotland:

A Reichian Reading of 1982, Janine

David Stenhouse

I FIRST encountered Alasdair Gray's novel *1982, Janine* in an unfortunate undergraduate class in 1988. Some of the women in the class had refused to read it at all, because they claimed it was pornography. The men who were brave enough to speak said that they had struggled to overcome the pornographic elements, but that they didn't understand the novel's politics. Inevitably the group broke up in confusion, but it had foundered on a real dilemma. Perhaps because in Scotland politics and sex seem to be very different activities, *1982, Janine* tends to be seen either as a political novel with embarrassing sexual elements, or as a sexual novel with dull political interruptions. Aside from this confusion there seems to be a general critical distaste about the book's 'pornographic' elements.[1] It's important to say simply that as pornography, *1982, Janine* is useless: it's almost impossible to imagine anyone being aroused by its fragmentary sexual storyline. Far from being pornography *1982, Janine* is a novel which takes as its subject all kinds of fantasy, including the pornographic. To characterise a novel which deals with pornography and fantasy as a piece of pornography itself is an example of critical and cultural illiteracy.

Pornography is material which has the straightforward, even banal aim of arousing the reader. The intention of *1982, Janine* is not nearly so simple. Early in the novel, Gray has his character Jock McLeish complain about the Marquis De Sade's habit of interrupting his sexual descriptions with long 'blethers' about the cruelty of nature. Rather than a sexual tale interrupted by political observations, Jock aims for a pornography which embraces history and politics:

> I will work like a historian describing in turn Germany Britain France Russia America China showing depression and dread growing within each for domestic reasons, but distracted by challenges and threats from abroad until the heads of government move to their controls in the hidden bunkers, and make

certain declarations, and then the tanks start rolling through
the streets with evacuations, concentration camps, explosions,
firestorms, frantic last minute propaganda and the awful to-
getherness of total calamity before the last, huge, final, bang.
That is how a big piece of pornography should go![2]

Even this bold credo doesn't explain why Scottish critics have such trouble with *1982, Janine*. In his introduction to *Gendering the Nation*, Christopher Whyte tries to provide one explanation by rhetorically asking: 'After all what (heterosexual) critic wants to put his (her) own fantasies on the line?'[3] I don't think that critics need to divulge their fantasy lives to engage with this book. They do need to follow the clues that *1982, Janine* provides in its vision of how pornography and politics are linked; of how sexual repression is connected to political repression. The book challenges its critics to find a conceptual framework in which to discuss those links. That framework can be be found in the work of the psychoanalyst Wilhelm Reich.

Alasdair Gray shows his knowledge of Wilhelm Reich in two ways. He acknowledges (in the List of Plagiarisms) that Reich inspired the Dragonhide in *Lanark* through his idea of character armour. Gray's other debt to Reich is even more important: *1982, Janine* draws its theme of the connection between sexual and political repression straight from Reich's writings. *1982, Janine* is the punctured interior monologue of Jock McLeish, an alcoholic installer of security installations, as he drinks and fantasizes during one night spent in a small Scottish hotel. For years Jock has been creating and developing an elaborate sexual fantasy incorporating shadowy secret installations where women are entrapped and forced to service sexually their male masters. The novel establishes a complex relationship between the personal and political, which is where Reich's work is so significant.

Reich's early psycho-analytical work was concerned with diagnosing the state of human sexuality under Capitalism. Reich believed that Capitalism ensures its survival by creating appropriately docile character structures in individuals. For Capitalism to survive, workers must have characters which are fearful, respectful of authority and sexually repressed. Repression guarantees that the workers fail to realise where their class interests lie. Reich's theory complements Gramsci's view of the ideological hegemony which exists under Capitalism, but goes further than Gramsci in stressing that those hegemonic ideas become internalised in human character itself. In *The Mass Psychology of Fascism* (1942) Reich notes that repressed sexuality 'inhibits the will to freedom':

sexual inhibition changes the structure of economically suppressed man in such a way that he acts, feels, and thinks contrary to his own material interests.[4]

These ideas are directly relevant to Gray's novel. *1982, Janine* disputes sexual and social regulation. Within Jock McLeish two ideologies, social authoritarianism and self-governing socialism, vie for dominance. As the text begins one system has been consigned by McLeish to the past, as a 'nice if it could work' political fantasy of socialist emancipation. The other is encoded as a sexual fantasy which fetishizes restraint. The novel shows McLeish in a traumatic debate with himself over which world view is correct. By the end of the night, and the novel, one complex political vision will be dominant.

The adult McLeish is identified with the power structure. His professional life is spent amongst business men, and his work safeguards the security of international companies and murky defence installations. His psychic identity has absorbed the political structures which characterises his working life to such an extent that even his name (McLeash) represents restraint and control. But Jock's life hasn't always been so repressed and fearful. He remembers a more hopeful past in which he believed that technology could be used for social emancipation. This dream is centred on his college friend Alan. McLeish remembers and idealises Alan as someone who was able to use technology to transform the everyday into the transcendent. Alan would have invented 'a delicate toylike structure'[5] which could provide domestic heat and light at no cost. He would work on Scottish society like 'a few ounces of yeast on many tons of malt'[6], and transform petrified social relationships. Appropriately, the period of greatest possibility in Jock's life is centred on an imaginative occasion. He works as an electrician on a theatrical show taken to the Edinburgh Festival. For a short time he is able to use technology creatively, to facilitate work of the imagination. Ironically, this period of imaginative possibility is ended by another fantasy. A brief sexual experience with Helen, one of the actresses in the play, results in what seems to be her pregnancy. Though she realises before the wedding that she is in fact not pregnant, the ceremony goes ahead. Jock's marriage and Alan's accidental death mark the end of most of Jock's hopes.

From this brief linking of technology to possibility and imagination McLeish has moved by the time the novel begins to fantasising about the various ways technology can be used as restraint. Since Jock's job involves installing security systems, his fantasy world draws on his professional life in ingenious ways. Despite, or because of, the implausible nature of Jock's fantasy, the technological details must be absolutely accurate to satisfy him, and so he uses his technical expertise freely. Accordingly, the diameter of an earring is given to the fraction of an inch, and a gearstick is imagined as capable of being folded down in order that a woman can be handcuffed to a car seat.

McLeish's sexual fantasies foreground the exercise of power and tie coercive force and sex to one another. The women in his fantasies, Janine, Superb, Helga and Big Momma, are employed by corporations which demand their literal or figurative enslavement and require performances from them which distort their behaviour. For McLeish the power to force people about or restrain them is sexy. The dramas played out in his fantasy are open about desire, envy, violence and sadism, while his public life conceals these feelings. His fantasy narratives are full of women whom he thinks of as wilful, sexual and greedy, women who do not conceal their emotions. Jock's fantasies fetishize restraint, yet ironically they allow full vent to the feelings that he restrains in his 'real' life.

The task of drawing on psycho-analytical ideas to make a literary analysis of *1982, Janine* is complicated by the fact that the novel displays a self-awareness about psycho-analytic theory. Jock has already been 'analysed' by Sontag, a lover from his 'real' life, who uses crude Freudian oppositions to dissect some of his fantasies. She attempts to reveal his potential homosexuality and explores the politics underlying his imaginary life. She also attempts to live out some of his fantasies, dressing up as Janine for him. In a decisive rejection of her strategy, Jock prefers his fantasy version. Sontag functions in the book as a symptom of resistance; by making Sontag an absurd figure Jock is trying to say that the whole notion of therapy is absurd. Nevertheless psycho-analytical theory can afford many insights into the novel. *1982, Janine* provides ample evidence of one of Reich's most fundamental concepts. Reich maintains that there is an equation between the stiff personality of a repressed person and their stiff uptight body. He suggests that repressed emotions are held in the body in muscular tensions and characteristic postures and gestures. He calls this structure Character Armour, the idea which inspired Dragonhide. *1982, Janine* is full of obsessive descriptions of bodies, but crucially not of Jock's own. Though we are told how Superb, Janine, Big Momma or Cupid look and dress we have no idea of the shape or characteristics of Jock's body. As if to emphasise his lack of interest in his own body McLeish even masturbates without using his hands. As a substitute for references to Jock's body we get references to his clothes; his tweed suit, his waistcoats, his bow ties all create an impression of a normal personality. Comparing himself to his friend Alan he notes: 'I walked with hands clasped behind my back. Alan usually had his arms folded on his chest but he did not strut or swagger'.[7] The restraint in his posture and body mirrors Jock's social restraint: 'I have never struck a man, woman or child in my life, never lost my temper, never raised my voice.' The text is also highly aware of the bodily characteristics of other characters. Jock is attracted to Helen by her 'sophisticated', rather aloof personality which is in fact a representation of her own fears; she is noted as holding herself as if she were cold during the rehearsals for the play. Against the tense, sexually reserved Jock and Helen are opposed a few characters who are sexually healthy. The most important of these characters is Denny. Jock remembers Denny as being sexually free. He recalls inadvertently having anal sex with her:

> 'Are you not sore?'
> 'No.'
> 'The books suggest it usually hurts the first time.'
> 'I don't read books.'[8]

Jock has got all the 'wrong' ideas about sex from books, films and jokes whilst Denny has not been socialised into conventional sexual fear. Reich noted that there were some 'genital characters' who had an uninhibited and healthy sexuality:

> There are human beings of a certain kind, living and working here and there, unobtrusively, who are equipped with natural sexuality; they are the genital characters. They are found frequently among the industrial workers.'[9]

Appropriately Denny comes from the proletariat. She has not internalised lower middle-class anxieties; her family structure is more diffuse, with an absent father and a mother who is often ill. She can be seen as a counterpoint to Helen whose parents are coldly conventional and snobbish. Jock agrees, in language strikingly similar to Reich's, that Denny is a 'natural' sexual being:

> There are such women. They are seldom glamorous or clever, they are not promiscuous, being usually married to self-satisfied chaps who do not notice why they are well-off...[10]

Reich suggests that whilst the family is the agency of authoritarian social enforcement, some families may be more authoritarian than others. Alan too is seen as being less conventional and socialised than Jock. This may be connected to his background, with a Jewish father and a 'tinker Irish' mother. Jock's own family was more conventional:

> I only once heard my parents laugh and never heard them raise their voices in anger, or complain or weep. The only one to

raise his voice in our house was Old Red when he denounced the capitalist class or talked Utopian, which was why Mum and I disliked him. We knew that most families were noisier than us, but also felt that noise was abnormal and unhealthy. We believed very few people were as normal and healthy as us.[11]

Jock and his mother equate repression and silence with health when in fact it signifies the opposite. Interestingly, the only person who disrupted the repressed quiet of Jock's parents was a socialist revolutionary friend of his father's, who aimed at overturning the whole social system. Later in the text Jock makes another allusion to his repressive childhood training. When Jock vomits up the pills which he had swallowed in an attempt to kill himself, he reflects that none of his sick missed the basin, thanks to 'early training'.[12]

Reich believed that one result of early training was to make the child ashamed of his sexuality. Jock agrees:

> ... most mothers teach their sons to be ashamed of their penis. I don't blame them. The churches teach us to be ashamed of our penis. They think our whole bodies are wicked.[13]

Reich placed great emphasis on the child's early sexual feelings. Jock describes how his sexual fantasies fitted easily into the domestic environment of his parents home.

> My mother was not a person but the climate I grew up in. All I remember about sex with her is, sitting on the opposite side of a room which felt like a prison (there was sunlight outside, down by the river the colliers' sons were guddling trout) a prison that gradually became more comfortable, expansive and palatial as I imagined the games I would play with Jane Russell when we were married.[14]

The passage flirts with Oedipal desire ('all I remember about sex with her') and has a highly ambivalent syntax: are the colliers' sons part of the 'sex' McLeish remembers? If so, it may explain why elsewhere in the novel McLeish equates his interest in the rough denim and dungarees that his female characters wear with the clothes that the colliers' sons wore when he was a child. In addition to this eroticisation of 'rough' maleness, McLeish's sexual fantasies have an infantile quality; the characters Big Momma (whom Jock is at pains to point out is not like his own mother) and the childlike Cupid clearly play upon an Oedipal theme. We can also see from this passage that as a boy Jock is already fantasizing about containment and restraint. The effect of Jock's 'early training' has been to turn his body itself into a kind of prison where tensions are held and never released. In an appropriately Reichian way, Jock even sites his feelings of pain and fear within his own body. At one point he dreams that he is lying in a bath, and picking the skin away from his ribcage: 'I could see only blackness inside but I knew it contained a rare work of art, a white ivory figure of a girl, obscenely mutilated.'[15] Later he asks: 'What is this ache inside me? It is pity, a slimy disgusting creature worming towards the surface of this face in order to split it open but by God it won't succeed.'[16] Later, as the pills Jock has swallowed begin to take hallucinogenic mental and textual effect, he articulates his feelings of physical restriction in a snatch of language: 'I can play no game in this tight suit.'[17]

Appropriately the transformation at the end of *1982, Janine* is tied to a physical release: for the first time since he was thirteen Jock is able to cry, and sheds tears for himself, his mother, Denny and Helen. In Reichian fashion, the release of an emotional block is tied to a physical change, and the tears release the feelings which have been physically repressed in the body.

In fact three physical emissions occur in the book, of semen, vomit and tears. The first and second are a matter of regret for Jock, the third is more significant and affords some relief. The vomiting stems from Jock's attempted suicide, which is the turning point of the book and is accompanied by the appearance and intervention of God. Though Jock tries to ignore Him, the voice of God insistently intrudes on his thoughts. Even here Gray is drawing on his knowledge of Reich. The intrusive God mirrors the intrusive Reichian therapist. Whereas the Freudian therapist listens to the patient, Reich proposed a more confrontational role for the therapist, who would debate, provoke and argue with the patient. The therapist might also physically manipulate the patient's body, applying pressure to those areas in which tension is being repressed. It is tempting to think that Jock's vomiting and tears are similarly due to such physical pressure.

After the physical release of the vomiting and his sleep, signified by two blank pages in the novel, Jock accelerates towards self-realisation. He pens a letter of resignation to his employers, the suggestively named National Securities Ltd, and looks forward to a life of greater freedom where he will be free of his feelings of fear. At the end of the novel the fantasy still exists, but Jock is not alienated from the characters it contains, seeing Janine as a reflection of his own identity. A Reichian would see Jock's fantasy as an elaborate fetish which held dammed up sexual energy. That energy would have been transformed by repression into an aggressive and sadistic fantasy which, despite its apparent aggression towards women, is actually directed against Jock. The novel would confirm this analysis since Jock notes that he gains his pleasure from identifying with his fantasy women at the moment when they realise they are trapped; his pleasure is masochistic rather than sadistic. If we accept that Jock's tears release pent up anxiety, then according to Reich the energy which has been held in his tense body will be available for more positive uses. The released energy could be used in a rational way by directing it against the society which demanded sexual repression in the first place. How will Jock's new state of being affect his politics?

Jock's Tory politics are seen as a sour product of his thwarted social and sexual relationships. Though Jock declares that he is a Conservative, he also makes incidental political observations which seem to come from a very different point of view. Leaving aside his eclectic comment that he is a Tory who accepts Marx, except 'the prophetic bit',[18] he also describes how little Denny earns, and notes that employers could afford to pay women working in catering badly because they had no trade union membership. His fantasies equate Janine with Scotland, and he declares that Scotland has been 'fucked'. His thoughts seem often to display Scottish Nationalist sympathies. Since Jock's Conservatism is tied in the text to his emotional and sexual repression, the implication is that like his sexual fantasies his politics is a type of neurosis, which might be unlocked.

If Jock's new state leads him to adopt a more rational political view, or even return to his earlier vision of socialist opportunity, he might find that his earlier vision of political possibility is rather like Reich's. Reich has a vivid vision of what a hopeful future could be like. He terms it 'work democracy':

> Every scientific person, whether he is an educator, lathe operator, technician, physician or something else, has to fulfil and safeguard the social work process. Socially he has a very responsible position. He has to prove each one of his assertions in a practical way. He has to work industriously, to think, to seek out new ways of improving his work, to recognise errors. As a researcher he has to examine and refute false theories... He has no need of power, for no motors can be constructed with political power, no sera can be produced with it, no children can be brought up, etc. The working scientific man lives and operates without weapons.[19]

That model, with its emphasis on the power of technology and technologists, its bypassing of existing political structures, its emphasis on hopeful social advance tied to scientific experimentation, is strikingly close to Jock's vision of the future as advanced in the theatrical section of *1982, Janine*. There technologists have the power to do away with famine and inequality, making existing political centres meaningless: Jock declares 'The centre of a properly lit land is everywhere'. Reich's vision of the responsibility of workers for their own work, of the significance of practical labour, have clear echoes in McLeish's and in Gray's vision.

Reich records that after therapy dislodged their physical repression of anxiety or pain, his patients regularly recovered

> a feeling of depth and earnestness, which was lost long ago ... patients recall that period in their early childhood in which the unity of their bodily sensations was as yet undisturbed. Deeply moved they relate how, as small children they felt one with nature with everything around them, they felt 'alive' ...[20]

Jock says:

> I will stand on the platform an hour from now, briefcase in hand, a neater figure than most but not remarkable. I will have the poise of an acrobat about to step onto the high wire, of an actor about to take the stage in a wholly new play. Nobody will guess what I am going to do. I do not know it myself. But I will not do nothing. No, I will not do nothing.[21]

The 'poise of an acrobat' is possible because McLeish's body has now expunged his pent up tensions. He may have re-achieved 'that period in [his] early childhood in which the unity of [his] bodily sensations was as yet undisturbed.' Throughout *1982, Janine* the connections between Gray's vision and Reich's are beguiling; even Jock's final credo 'It is ideas that make people brave, ideas and love of course'[22] resembles the motto of Reich's Orgone Foundation: 'Love, work and knowledge are the well-springs of our life. They should also govern it.' It is appropriate that the visionary Gray has drawn on the work of the visionary Reich to propose a view of politics and sex which disrupts conventional expectation. In the process, he has pointed Jock McLeish and the reader towards a vision of a wholly healthy Scotland.

Notes

1. This distaste dominates S. J. Boyd's 'Black Arts: *1982, Janine* and *Something Leather*', in Crawford and Nairn (eds.), *The Arts of Alasdair Gray* (Edinburgh: 1991).
2. Alasdair Gray, *1982, Janine* (London: 1984), p. 29.
3. Christopher Whyte (ed.), 'Introduction', *Gendering the Nation* (Edinburgh: 1995).
4. Wilhelm Reich, *The Mass Psychology of Fascism* (New York: 1970), p. 32.
5. *Janine*, p. 265.
6. ibid, p. 108.

7. ibid, p. 109.
8. ibid, p. 106.
9. Wilhelm Reich, *The Function of the Orgasm* (London: 1968), p. 171.
10. *Janine*, p.212.
11. ibid, p. 197.
12. ibid, p. 186.
13. ibid, p. 49.
14. ibid, p. 50.
15. ibid, p. 132.
16. ibid, p. 146.
17. ibid, p. 182.
18. ibid, p. 62.
19. *Mass Psychology of Fascism*, p. 365.
20. *Function of the Organism*, p. 319.
21. *Janine*, p. 341.
22. ibid, p. 340.

David Stenhouse presents the BBC Radio Scotland arts programme *The Usual Suspects*. He is currently completing a Ph.D. thesis on John Crowe Ransom.

Without secrecy there would be no pornography.
Pornography and Obscenity, D. H. Lawrence, 1929)

In the realm of Scottish literary criticism, so preoccupied with the issue of identity, it needs to be acknowledged that in our twentieth-century world all identity starts with the individual's definition of him or herself. Naturally, questions of sexuality and gender make up a crucial part of one's identity. But wereas women and gays – keen to reach a fulfilling definition of their place in society – can never avoid a confrontation with the strai(gh)tjacket of traditional gender roles, heterosexual men have so far managed to do without such a confrontation which would involve a profound re-consideration of all one's attitudes towards sexuality and gender.
Berthold Schoene in *Gendering the Nation*, Edinburgh, 1995

Unspeakable Heterosexuality

Christopher Whyte

IN AUTUMN 1993 I received a letter from the managing editor of *Scotlands* asking me for a piece on Scotland and sexuality for the gender issue of the journal. Pressure of work meant that I could not possibly agree to supply the material within the time stipulated and I wrote an enjoyably mischievous reply suggesting, for reasons which will become apparent, that several members of the editorial board were in a better position to write on the subject. While turning the request down with an almost clear conscience, I was aware of a lingering sense of dissatisfaction. Had I chickened out? If I was honest with myself, I had found it inconvenient for more than practical reasons. Why had *Scotlands* thought of me for such a problematic topic? Did the board imagine I had some privileged insight into sexuality denied to a range of other possible contributors? And how could anyone cope with such an impossible remit?

My suspicion was that they had fixed on me because I was known to be gay. Indeed, I was one of an extremely limited group of Scottish writers and critics who make no secret of the fact (though emerging from the closet is a process that never seems to end), and are prepared to admit in print to practising the love that dare(d) not speak its name. Gay and lesbian people are defined, in the minds of others if not in our own, by our sexualities. It is the crucial component in our make up and we may therefore be perceived as more intensely sexual than the 'normal' majority (even if promiscuity is no less constrictive a stereotype for gay men than chastity was for Victorian women). This, I thought, might explain the unusual honour *Scotlands* had paid me.

But my reflections did not stop there. The sexuality I practise has a longstanding and intimate connection with silence. A silence of what kind? Foucault insists on the multiple nature of silence, its constant implication with discourse:

> Silence itself – the things one declines to say, or is forbidden to name, the discretion that is required between different speakers – is less the absolute limit of discourse, the other side from which it is separated by a strict boundary, than an element

which functions alongside the things said, with them and in relation to them within over-all strategies. There is no binary division to be made between what one says and what one does not say; we must try to determine the different ways of not saying such things... There is not one but many silences.[1]

The silence around homosexuality was, until recently, so scandalous that to admit its existence, even in a whisper, would have been as deafening as a thunderclap. (When I told a fellow academic of the coming-out interview I had conducted with Edwin Morgan in October 1989,[2] he commented in wonder: 'Does that mean it can be talked about?') Such was its power of contagion and corruption that merely to name homosexuality was to infringe a taboo, never mind admitting to its practice or proselytising for its inherent pleasurability.

The forbidden acquires an allure by the very fact of being proscribed. One of the many paradoxes of homophobia (an infinitely more puzzling object of study than homosexuality itself) is that it perceives intragender sex as a threat precisely because it is immensely pleasurable and is entirely divorced from the procreative imperative. Who, having tasted of forbidden fruit, would choose to go back to simple, everyday fare? So one must not name the fruit, far less discuss its current availability on the market. Perceptions of this kind underlie British legislation against the 'promotion' of homosexuality. They continue to render the existence of gay and lesbian teachers (though not, I trust, gay lecturers) precarious.

My concern was that *Scotlands* was asking me to collude in a different silence, the silence about 'normality', the silence of those who claim to be, or consider themselves 'normal'. My discursive position was sexed and gendered from the outset in a way the position of other possible contributors, and of members of the editorial board, was (to my knowledge) not. Was I being asked to act by proxy, to assist them in the painful transition from a universalist stance (which was in fact, at various times, and sometimes simultaneously, male, heterosexual, Scottish, white, middle-class and, why not, Protestant) to one which acknowledged its own partiality, its limited validity? Or was I being asked to write about Scotland and sexuality because if others did so the transition would have been forced on them willy-nilly? Because they would have had to call their own bluff and step down from the soapbox of normality? If those who broke the silence about homosexuality were in the past punished with scandal and ostracisation, breaking the silence about 'normality' would involve a voluntary abdication of power.

The harsh truth is that, in a world where identities are defined through difference, the 'normal' does not exist. In so far as any sexuality succeeds in bidding for 'normal' status, it remains both invisible and unspeakable. To write with any effectiveness about Scotland and sexuality I would have had to break someone else's silence, to render the 'normal', 'identical' sexuality imputed to the mass of men and women in Scotland visible and speakable. Yet the only speakable forms of heterosexuality are the perverse ones.

Foucault relates the development of a Western discourse on sexuality to the practice of the confessional. In a sacrament of which I personally have direct and painful experience (thankfully, now in the distant past), the obligation to disclose is not indiscriminate. Only transgressions need be articulated. Oh for those heady days when one racked one's brains for something to confess while waiting one's turn! A blameless existence conducted according to God's dictates issues in silence. To be 'normal' is to have nothing to say. The right to speech on sexuality is a privilege of the perverse: potentially everyone's, in other words.

I never cease to be fascinated by the way traditional narrative patterns place marriage at the close. If you are a character in a book, getting married is a kind of narrative suicide. Your story stops there. Nothing more can be said about you and you disappear from the pages of the text. As Akhmatova has it:

> And in books it was the last page
> I preferred to all the others –
> When the hero and heroine
> Are no longer interesting,
> And so many years have passed
> That no one is pitiful anymore,
> And, it seems, the author
> Has by now forgotten the start of the story...[3]

Of course she is absolutely right. But why are the hero and heroine 'no longer interesting' once they have got married? The heterosexual relationship of partnership and parenthood which founds a 'normal' family is put forward as the constituent element of our society, its moral and reproductive backbone. It structures relations of power around gender and sexuality. Its importance is such that, like the human form in mosques, it must not be represented. There is too much at stake for stories to circulate about it. Courtship, marital breakdown, infidelity, bereavement, are all acceptable subjects for stories. The party can be discussed before it starts or once it has broken up. But while it is on, silence has to be observed. A 'normal', functioning heterosexual relationship is excluded from our traditional narrative canons. It is omnipotent, omnipresent and unrepresentable.

Perhaps the nearest one gets to it is a child's narrative about its parents, characterised by silence and exclusion, by what the child cannot or should not know. We are all supposed to originate from such a relationship, in more than purely biological terms. According to Foucault, psychoanalysis sees the parents' relationship as the core of the individual psyche, almost as if individuality were a telescope that, raised to the eye, reveals a heterosexual coupling which alone accounts for its genesis:

> psychoanalysis, whose technical procedure seemed to place the confession of sexuality outside family jurisdiction, rediscovered the law of alliance, the involved workings of marriage and kinship, and incest at the heart of this sexuality, as the principle of its formation and the key to its intelligibility.[4]

From an early age the married couple is pointed out to us as not only our origin but also our ideal destination. A destination, however, which cannot be narrated. How could I, still testing out the words and phrases that can express my own sexuality, assume the task of making 'normal' sexuality visible? Of speaking its name? And if it is now, at last, in my interests to speak, could it be in the interests of the 'normal' to maintain their silence? Or at least, to delegate the task of breaking it to others?

Such binary divisions of sexuality along axes like normal/abnormal, sanctioned/transgressive or even heterosexual/homosexual have a limited usefulness:

> categories presented in a culture as symmetrical binary oppositions – heterosexual/homosexual, in this case – actually subsist in a more unsettled and dynamic tacit relation according to which, first, term B is not symmetrical with but subordinated to term A; but, second, the ontologically valorized term A actually depends for its meaning on the simultaneous subsumption and exclusion of term B; hence, third, the question of priority between the supposed central and the supposed marginal category of each dyad is irresolvably unstable, an instability caused by the fact that term B is constituted as at once internal and external to term A.[5]

The way women are subsumed within terms such as 'men' or 'he', only to be divided off from men in other contexts, is symptomatic of this instability. At times the male pronoun stands for all human beings, at others only for those who are biologically male. The boundary between the two usages is fluid and imprecise. The female reader faces a repeated enigma of inclusion and exclusion.

Though superficially they privilege the dominant term, these oppositions betray its cognitive dependence on the subordinate one. If you want to know what masculinity is, first examine the nature of femininity, the 'marked' term. Masculinity is traditionally defined as its absence. It is the unknown which subsists in a space from which the known has been eliminated. It is originary, axiomatic and indefinable.

Heterosexuality has a similarly enigmatic quality, for the concept of a unified and normative heterosexuality is highly problematic. Nancy Chodorow, writing from a psychological standpoint, asks whether it makes sense to group heterosexual men and women under the same term:

> A woman's choice of a male sexual object or lover is typically so different – developmentally, experientially, dynamically, and in its meaning for her womanliness and femininity – from a man's choice of a femal sexual object or lover that it is not at all clear whether we should identify these by the same term. We can do so behaviorally and definitionally – a hetero-object is other than or different from the self, whereas a homo-subject is like the self – and there is certainly a culturally normative distinction that conflates heterosexuals of both genders, but we may thereby confuse our psychological understanding.[6]

With similar imprecision, the heterosexual/homosexual opposition leads us to group the sexuality of a gay male couple under the same heading as that of a lesbian couple. Yet are they in any sense identical phenomena? In so far as sexualities are not two but multiple, the existence of a 'majority', 'normal' sexuality cannot be posited in any but the most crudely statistical terms (in an area where statistics are notoriously unreliable).

In the binary division of sexuality, why has such overwhelming importance been attributed to the identity or difference of genders? Why have other distinctions been sidelined, such as those who engage in sexual activity as against those who have little or none, those who prefer sex with other people as against those who would rather play with themselves, those who are happy with one partner as against those who feel the need for several, either sequentially or concurrently? Chodorow comes up with a possible answer when she observes that the two factors common to all psychoanalytic narratives of the genesis of heterosexuality are gender inequality and male dominance.[7] It is power relations between the genders that have given heterosexuality its determining role. Does this mean that, in a society where men and women were truly equal, heterosexuality as we know it would cease to exist?

I wrote about the silence around homosexuality in an early sequence of poems. It was both a passport to immunity ('Is thubhairt mi rium fhìn: ma bhitheas tu/ balbh, is dòcha nach mothaichear dhut', 'And I said to myself "If you keep/ quiet, maybe they won't notice you"') and 'toirmeasg an àigh/ a dhùin mo bheul, a thug orm a bhith balbh', 'a ban to joy that closed/ my mouth, and forced me to be dumb'.[8] Edwin Morgan broke the silence in his poetry not through a sign, but through the absence of a sign, a refusal to specify the gender of the addressee in his love lyrics. Despite the clear phallic imagery and the careful clue supplied in the first line (what is the hidden source? what originates the poem yet cannot be shown?) there is little doubt that 'One Cigarette' was read by many, in the two decades after its first appearance, as a 'normal' love poem:

> No smoke without you, my fire.
> After you left,
> your cigarette glowed on in my ashtray
> and sent up a long thread of such quiet grey
> I smiled to wonder who would believe its signal
> of so much love. One cigarette
> in the non-smoker's tray.
> As the last spire
> trembles up, a sudden draught
> blows it winding into my face.
> Is it smell, is it taste?
> You are here again, and I am drunk on your tobacco lips.
> Out with the light.
> Let the smoke lie back in the dark.
> Till I hear the very ash
> sigh down among the flowers of brass
> I'll breathe, and long past midnight, your last kiss.[9]

Morgan's ambivalence is not merely a consequence of self-censorship or discretion. His love lyrics are multiple texts which neatly elude the oppositions male/female or heterosexual/homosexual and offer themselves to a range of readings none of which can definitely exclude any other. The tactic was no less powerful than the most outspoken of declarations and perhaps more longlasting in its destabilising effects.[10]

The breaking of each of the silences, about homosexuality and about heterosexuality, has different implications. For a gay man to declare himself is an act of disobedience, a movement into visibility bringing with it the threat of violence which most women face on a daily basis by the very fact of their gender. It is an assertion of our right to exist, our right to speak and be spoken about. It claims discursive space. In so far as the 'normal' fails to suffocate such voices, its own territory shrinks. Recognising the existence of subjects it does not represent, the 'normal' position can no longer claim universal validity. Its practice of exclusion becomes explicit.

What about breaking the other silence, the silence about 'normality'? Chodorow is concerned, not with literary texts, but with psychoanalytic accounts. Here, too, she comes up against the absence of a narrative about the norm, against the silence in which it subsists:

> because heterosexuality has been assumed, its origins and vicissitudes have not been described: psychoanalysis does not have a developmental account of 'normal' heterosexuality (which is, of course, a wide variety of heterosexualities) that compares in richness and specificity to accounts we have of the development of the various homosexualities and what are called perversions.

Binary oppositions again prove inherently unstable when, on the same page, Chodorow confesses that:

> after Freud, most of what one can tease out about the psychoanalytic theory of 'normal' heterosexuality comes about by reading between the lines in writings on perversions and homosexuality.[11]

If you want to know what makes a heterosexual, you must first find out what makes a homosexual. The privileged term depends for its meaning on the subordinate term. It can, in fact, be argued that the invention of the heterosexual was a consequence of the invention of the homosexual and took place at a later date.

Kosofsky Sedgwick is uncertain whether or not 'this silent, normative, uninterrogated "regular" heterosexuality' in fact functions as a sexuality at all:

> The making historically visible of heterosexuality is difficult because, under its institutional pseudonyms such as Inheritance, Marriage, Dynasty, Family, Domesticity, and Population, heterosexuality has been permitted to masquerade so fully as History itself – when it has not presented itself as the totality of Romance.[12]

That masquerading as history, that occupation of all the available discursive space, has been made possible by the two silences. On the one hand, the silence imposed on a 'perverse' homosexuality has allowed the 'normal' establishment to misrepresent the sexualities of past ages, while dreaming of a world without queers. On the other, the silence about heterosexuality has disguised its internal contradictions. Even if one were to concede it self-identity (and that is problematic), it would be merely one among a range of manifestations of human sexuality so far known to us.

Since heterosexuality is not one, a straight woman's relation to the silence about it is different from a straight man's. I heard Liz

Lochhead read her poem 'What the Pool Said, On Midsummer's Day'[13] at a book launch in the original Edinburgh Waterstone's many years ago. Her courage and outspokenness filled me with admiration. How could a Scottish woman dare to read such a sexually explicit poem in front of a conventionally respectable audience? When I return to the poem now, I find it unsatisfactory on several counts, since it voices not the woman's experience but the man's fear. The pool articulates, agrees to personify many of the most hackneyed stereotypes of femininity. It is 'garrulous', 'dark/ and still and deep'. Even the brilliant sunshine cannot 'white me out'. It is 'inviting, winking' and has been known to 'flash and dazzle', to deploy 'zazzing dragonflies' so as to lure the man closer. It is water and woman, 'fish' to the man's 'flesh', 'wet weeds' against his thigh. A lesbian relationship pales into insignificance against the challenge, the collision between genders:

> The woman was easy.
> Like to like, I called to her, she came.
> In no time I had her
> out of herself, slipping on my water-stockings,
> leaning into, being cupped and clasped
> in my green glass bra.
> But it's you I want, and you know it, man.

By the third paragraph the poem is focusing unambiguously on what it is like for him, not what is happening for her. The pool enthusiastically subscribes to age-old truisms that identify femininity with unreason and prehistory:

> Your reasonable fear,
> what's true in me admits it.
> (Though deeper, oh
> older than any reason.)

The 'true' elements in the pool predate the advent of reason and leap to validate the man's fear, to identify with his experience. The poem illustrates the difficulties a straight woman faces in breaking the silence about 'normal' sexuality. It is a disturbing instance of projective identification. Rather than finding a female voice, Lochhead agrees to act out male projections, to be what men have claimed that women are. It is as if she stepped into a ready made mould, doing all she can to make it move and speak.

I raise the issue of projective identification (I become what you perceive me to be) because I have encountered it in my own work. The poem 'Rex tenebrarum'[14] moves from a wounded acceptance of the traditional religious stance, associating my sexuality with the devil, since it cannot be with God, and it led me into a trap from which I did my best to escape thanks to the image of the seed and a redefining of the diabolical:

> Mura bi eòl aig a' ghais
> air stèidheachadh nam freumh,
> 's am fàs gu lèir ag aideachadh
> gur ann bhon dorchadas a thig
> gach uile mhaoin is beathachadh,
> mura bi gaol neo-mhealltach aige
> air na ghin 's na dh'àraich e,
> ciamar a thig ar dòchasan
> fo dheagh bhàrr samhradh blàthachaidh?
>
> *Unless the sapling knows*
> *where its roots are sunk, and the whole*
> *plant admits that life*
> *and nourishment come from darkness;*
> *unless it has unequivocal*
> *love for what bore and raised it*
> *how can there be a rich*
> *summer flowering for our hopes?*

Morgan skilfully avoided such pitfalls by camouflage, by writing lyrics which could, at a pinch, apply to a heterosexual or a homosexual situation, eluding the gender double bind. Given the enthusiasm with which 'What the Pool Said, On Midsummer's Day' buys into binary oppositions, it is hardly surprising that it should fall a victim to the trap of projective identification.

One cannot base a critique of a poet's work on the reading of a single poem, however significant. Nevertheless, it does raise important questions about Lochhead's popularity, her palatability to the male establishment. Does she represent, on the Scottish scene, a form of feminism men can deal with? Is one of the attractions of her work its comforting familiarity? And is this a consequence of the fact that, rather than offering a new voice, she duplicates the traditional one, confirming its claims while appearing to challenge them? There can be little doubt that her promotion to the literary pantheon has soothed the consciences of many a male establishment figure and provided them with a superficial gender credibility they might otherwise have lacked.

It would appear that a straight man can only break the silence about heterosexuality by rendering it perverse. This is what occurs in two crucial and closely interrelated texts about Scottish masculinity, Hugh MacDiarmid's *A Drunk Man Looks at the Thistle* and Alasdair Gray's *1982 Janine*.[15] Both present the reader with a tormented masculinity, one that cannot accept itself and invites the reader to challenge it, to dissociate from it. Where the fiction of

Gunn and McIlvanney engages in a species of gender Kailyard, deploying all its arts of seduction to win our assent to the glorification of the hero, MacDiarmid and Gray offer the uncomfortable spectacle of a masculinity which is self-confessedly pathological, and make an implicit demand that we envisage some alternative. Jock McLeish announces at the core of Gray's novel that 'I am shit' (p.129), and the idea of reading MacDiarmid's poem *with* the Drunk Man rather than against him is almost too horrific to contemplate. Both texts constitute an indictment of the attitudes they embody. If internal evidence were not enough, MacDiarmid's words to George Ogilvie, contrasting the *Drunk Man* and *To Circumjack Cencrastus*, indicate his distance from the earlier poem:

> But where the *Drunk Man* is in one sense a reaction from the 'Kailyard', *Cencrastus* transcends that altogether – the Scotsman gets rid of the thistle, 'the bur o' the world' – and his spirit at last inherits its proper sphere. Psychologically it represents the resolution of the sadism and masochism, the synthesis of the various sets of antitheses I was posing in the *Drunk Man*. It will not depend on the contrasts of realism and metaphysics, bestiality and beauty, humour and madness – but move on a plane of pure beauty and pure music.[16]

The passage almost prompts one to dub the *Drunk Man* an *Inferno* in contrast to the planned *Paradiso* of *To Circumjack Cencrastus*. MacDiarmid can even be cast as a Lacanian before his time, for *A Drunk Man* interestingly formulates while it consciously parodies certain basic elements of Lacan's teaching. The phallus is omnipresent, structuring reality on a series of different planes. It is not just Yggdrasil, the world tree holding up the sky, but also the crucifix, the core image of New Testament Christianity, as well as the thistle, the symbol of Scottish nationhood. The poem's closing section constitutes an outburst of gendered megalomania. The erect thistle/phallus sustains the vault of heaven and the hero manages to spray the stars with his ejaculation. Creativity is presented in quintessentially male terms as an outpouring followed by detumescence and the horror of an absence, a vacuum:

> The stars like thistle's roses floo'er
> The sterile growth o' Space ootour,
> That clad in bitter blasts spreids oot
> Frae me, the sustenance o' its root.
>
> O fain I'd keep my hert entire,
> Fain hain the licht o' my desire,
> But ech! the shinin' streams ascend,
> And leave me empty at the end.

> For aince it's toomed my hert and brain,
> The thistle needs maun fa' again.
> – But a' its growth 'll never fill
> The hole it's turned my life intill! (lines 2659-2670)

The end of erection, the collapse of the thistle means the Drunk Man has lost the sign which dissociated him from the feminine, from a gap which is both tomb and womb:

> *Thistleless fule,*
> You'll ha'e nocht left
> But the hole frae which
> *Life's struggle is reft!...* (lines 529-532)

Writing to the sculptor Pittendrigh Macgillivray, MacDiarmid was perfectly frank about 'the objectionable elements' in his poem and willing to acknowledge them as part of his own personal make-up.[17] The fantasies of humiliation and entrapment which crop up repeatedly in the pages of *1982 Janine* are crucial to the text and any attempt to apologise for them, excuse them or sanitise them is misguided. They are an integral part of Gray's decision to speak from the position of a heterosexual man. He could only break the silence by stepping down from the pedestal of normality. To be spoken, to be made visible, the norm had to be rendered perverse.

Foucault characteristically declines to take a simplistic attitude to power, whereby the powerful would be evil and oppressive and the powerless victims but good. Power, he writes:

> is the moving substrate of force relations which, by virtue of their inequality, constantly engender states of power, but the latter are always local and unstable... power is not an institution, and not a structure; neither is it a certain strength we are endowed with; it is the name that one attributes to a complex strategical situation in a particular society.[18]

Rightly or wrongly, I viewed the editorial board of *Scotlands* as part of the heterosexual establishment, asking me to break a silence they themselves, for strategical reasons, preferred to maintain. But the upshot of my reflections was to see myself as empowered and the 'normal' position as powerless. The price of normality (or of its attribution) is silence, is having nothing interesting to say. Normality is a facade which both privileges and inhibits. If one is to have a story, to be in possession of a narrative others will wish to hear, one must emerge from behind that facade. Because, in the end, an acknowledgement of reciprocity is the condition for all speech.

Notes
1. Michel Foucault *The History of Sexuality Vol. 1: An Introduction* translated Robert Hurley (London, Penguin 1990) p. 27.
2. 'Power from things not declared' in Edwin Morgan *Nothing not giving messages* (Edinburgh, Polygon 1990) pp. 144–187.
3. *The Complete Poems of Anna Akhmatova* translated by Judith Hemschemeyer, edited and introduced by Roberta Reeder (Somerville, Massachusetts, Zephyr Press 1990) Vol. 1 pp. 167, 169.
4. Foucault p. 113.
5. Eve Kosofsky Sedgwick *Epistemology of the Closet* (Hemel Hempstead, Harvester Wheatsheaf 1991) pp. 9–10.
6. Nancy J. Chodorow *Femininities Masculinities Sexualities: Freud and Beyond* (London, Free Association Books 1994) pp. 35–6.
7. Ibid. p. 35.
8. Crisdean Whyte *Uirsgeul/Myth: Poems in Gaelic with English translations* (Glasgow, Gairm 1991) pp. 4–7.
9. Edwin Morgan *The Second Life* (Edinburgh, Edinburgh University Press 1968) p. 63.
10. See in this connection my '"Now you see it, now you don't": Revelation and Concealment in the Love Poetry of Edwin Morgan' in *The Glasgow Review* 2 Gender (Autumn 1993) pp. 82–93.
11. Chodorow p. 34.
12. Eve Kosofsky Sedgwick *Tendencies* (London, Routledge 1994) pp. 10–11.
13. Liz Lochhead *Dreaming Frankenstein and Collected Poems* (Edinburgh, Polygon 1984) pp. 8–9.
14. *Uirsgeul/Myth* pp. 64–9.
15. Hugh MacDiarmid *A Drunk Man Looks at the Thistle* edited Kenneth Buthlay (Edinburgh, Scottish Academic Press 1987), Alasdair Gray *1982 Janine* (Harmondsworth, Penguin 1985).
16. *The Letters of Hugh MacDiarmid* edited with an introduction by Alan Bold (London, Hamish Hamilton 1984) p. 91.
17. Ibid. p. 322.
18. Foucault p. 93.

Once in a hot courtroom in New Zealand, I had occasion to ask a lady who was giving evidence against me for saying 'fuck' in a public meeting, whether she was as disgusted and offended by hearing the word 'rape' used in a similar context. She wasn't. I asked her why. She thought for a moment and said happily, 'Because for rape the woman doesn't give her consent.'
Seduction is a Four-Letter Word, Germaine Greer, 1973

Ourselves as Others:

Marabou Stork Nightmares

Alan Freeman

WHAT GOES AROUND comes around. From its traditionally perceived problems in addressing fractured personal, social and linguistic reality, fiction in Scotland has flourished in recent times, formal innovation and confidence of voice marking the progress of ever more authors. None has shown more confidence than Irvine Welsh, and no-one has reached a wider audience. Yet for all its swagger, Welsh's work exhibits lavish qualities of the spiritual despair and fractured identity so frequently found in Scottish fiction over the years. Welsh leads us in exciting new directions, but, especially in his second novel, *Marabou Stork Nightmares*[1], we may be heading up Cripple Creek.

Even the most realistic novel is more a reflection of the artist's imagination than a record of how reality is. Scottish reality suffers the 'fracture, disintegration and damaged identity' associated with late capitalism the world over, but pre-occupation in novels with the crippled spirit is itself entrenched as a readily identifiable motif, all too easily assimilable in writing.[2] Its perpetuation is our deepest modern cultural stereotype, and is as much symptom as diagnosis of cultural self-hate. In his ultra-realist writing, Welsh exemplifies the strengths and weaknesses of this motif.

Roy Strang lies comatose in a hospital bed following a failed suicide attempt. As he slowly returns to consciousness, we are inside his mind. He enacts a quest to kill the Marabou Storks which stalk flamingoes in a South African safari park. But as his coma subsides, Strang is less able to evade his memory, and fantasy is influenced by, and gives way to, recollection of the events which led to his overdose. Strang recounts his childhood in Edinburgh, interspersed with a brief emigration to South Africa, his escalating teenage violence, leading him into the Hibs Casuals, and to his participation in a brutal gang rape. By the time the reader learns this, the rape victim has caught up with Strang to exact her own violent revenge.

Maintaining a consistent narrative framework on this scale is new to Welsh, and he approaches it boldly. But while there is much audacity and imagination in the book, there are also many unsatisfactory features, leaving questions about its achievement. The narrative structure, moving between fantasy and realist accounts of Strang's life, and with much typographical variation, seems derivative of both Alasdair Gray and Iain Banks. From seeming a bizarre alternative world, though, the fantasy sequences quickly resolve into Strang's contrived escapist imaginings. His invented character Lockhart Dawson remarks that 'the role of ritual is to make things safe for those who have most to lose by things not being safe' (p.44), but the African adventures of Roy and his chum Sandy Jamieson are constantly impinged on by the darker elements of fear, guilt and self-loathing. Seeking refuge in abstraction, neither escape nor atonement are possible, and images of abuse force their way into the Boys' Own registers Strang adopts. Implicit in these is the power relation underpinning those old schoolboys' yarns, the jolly surface of imperial culture. As with the rest of the book though, these passages are ingenious and tedious in equal measure, detailing the inner processes of Roy's troubled mind, but their sexual references are simplistic and predictable. It's an old joke by now: wholesome surface, healthy lads together, Enid Blyton and *The Valiant*, but with allusions to lurking homosexuality or racism:

> I feel a cool breeze in my face and turn to face my companion. He's in good spirits behind the wheel of our jeep.
> – You've been at the wheel far too long, Sandy. I'll take over! I volunteered.
> – Wizard! Sandy replied, pulling over by the side of the dusty track.
> A large insect settled on my chest. I swatted the blighter. – Yuk! Those insects, Sandy! How positively yucky!
> – Absolutely, he laughed, clambering over into the back of the vehicle. – It'll be great to stretch these damn pins! He smiled, extending his long, tanned muscular legs across the back seat.
> (p.4)

If the Boys' Own register was sustained with any success there might be more mileage in such a passage. Though Strang is attempting the style and failing to sustain it here, the penetration by his greater fears removes any subtlety. All that 'wizard', 'blighter' and 'positively yucky!' overdoes the tone of private-school-boyish glee, and the sexual innuendo is no more than cliché. Increasingly, the fantasy sequences become exercises in how bad Strang is at parodying adventure formats.

While the life of the Hibs Casuals is portrayed elsewhere in the book, the fantasy sequences embody the business jungle surrounding the game. And a gross body it is too, in the shape of an ugly, abusive chairman intent on take-over. All right-minded individuals will be cheered by the references to Emerald Park withstanding the ambitions of the ignoble neighbouring Jambola and its corpulent corporate head, Dawson Lockhart. But again, other than a running joke for football fans, this contributes little to the development of the novel. Laughter mingles with disgust at the image of the well-known chairman applying lubricating jelly to his penis, in preparation to force himself on a boy slave (p.219), but such caricature is too pervasive, restricting the scope of the work. Even this level of grossness becomes banal. Where the novel does score, following good approach work, is in the central image of Sandy Jamieson, or Jimmy Sandison, and the Marabou Stork. The injustice suffered by the real Jimmy Sandison in a real football match, seen on video by Strang as he lapses into his coma, is revealed as the trigger for his Jambola safari:

> I wanted to help him, I wanted to help all the people who'd ever suffered injustices, even though it was just a fuckin recorded tape of a fitba match I was watching. I'd never seen a man so shocked and outraged at such an obvious miscarriage of sporting justice. (p.255)

A motif for an unjust world to which Strang has made his own, terrible contribution, from this insight the strands of the narrative follow, occasionally merging in references to diamonds (the gems mined in South Africa, the song sung by his mother, the fitba team from Airdrie). Strang's evolving vision of the predatorial Marabou Stork is his perception of a frightening world and the self which he has inhabited within it; both the cruelty Strang has suffered and the demon within him. Offshoots of this imagery occurring throughout the narrative add richly to its texture, including the marabou shapes and the Z representing the Zero Tolerance campaign against violence to women initiated by Edinburgh District Council, suggested in the typographical arrangement.

More familiar to followers of Welsh are the realist portions of the narrative, couched in Edinburgh dialect, which tell of the narrator's development. The family's sojourn to South Africa provides an interesting reminder of the ambivalent status of Scots, as colonisers and colonised, reflecting the relativism of power and powerlessness which is always present in Welsh's work. We see in this the cycles of abuse found in a dysfunctional family living in, by implication, a dysfunctional community. Another sub-genre of Scottish fiction, this is the bildungsroman of the sensitive soul suffering in an insensitive environment, where the patriarch is chief tormentor.

On the question of realism, we find ourselves in the territory that made Welsh's debut novel *Trainspotting* so striking. Few writers have such an ear for speech, from the rhythms of accent to the patterns of rhetoric we unconsciously employ and which betray our habitual outlook as well as particular emotions. John Strang's paranoia is restrained for much of his representation within a credible if insistent series of vocal gestures. Repeating key phrases and surrounding them with his characteristic 'like ah sais', John demonstrates his ongoing attempt to stabilise his own identity. But the flux remains, and it's this continual oscillation between fixing experiences in language, and their slide away from signification, that Welsh seems to grasp effortlessly:

> Dad stood up and went over to the window. His voice took on a compulsive mocking bent as he thumbed over his shoulder at the outside world. – Ah ken whit they cunts think ay us. Ah ken aw they cunts. Ken what they are? Ah'll fuckin well tell ye what they are, he slurred, – Rubbish. Not fuckin quoted. That's these cunts: not fuckin quoted. (p.149)

And yet John must keep attributing attitudes and speech to aw they cunts. Identity is not founded on stability but is a relative condition; in this case the Strang name is based emphatically on us and them relations, John Strang evoking the external 'other' in order to define himself. That he does so while basing his sense of self on received quotations from Winston Churchill and images of war assist in this patterning; but that he is ultimately dependent upon the 'other' to attain a sense of himself is the irony of such paranoia. Through language we undergo a flow in self-identification, words passing from the external world into inner experience, and back. The more unstable John becomes the more desperately he needs those external others, imagined enemies to reach out to strike at.

Likewise the narrator Roy Strang. For the young Roy, agony is piled on shame, as sexual and violent child abuse are added to the catalogue of his physical and psychological woes. Estranged from himself and from the world outside, he fights to assert his name:

> ah turned tae the half-emptied pub, only maist ae them were shitein it tae, wi Norrie and Jacksie oan the door an ah shouted, - ROY STRANG'S THE FUCKIN NAME! REMEMBER THAT FUCKIN NAME! ROY STRANG! HIBS BOYS YA FUCKIN CUNTS! (p.172)

The Strangs more than most sense the flux of identity and language. You live in your name, but the name is never fixed. However strang you are, you're always pretty strange too. And in the fictional vision of Irvine Welsh, the real is always on the verge of collapsing before you.

But where in *Trainspotting* the flux of language and social being draw the reader sympathetically in to the plight of its inhabitants, *Marabou Stork Nightmares* lacks this depth and tenderness. Caricature replaces the creative grotesquerie that made Spud and Renton so memorable in *Trainspotting*. In that novel, Welsh locates his characters on the social margin, but challenges his readers with their humanity. Consider Spud's reaction to his friends attacking a squirrel on the Meadows:

> Sick Boy's nearest tae it, n tries tae entice it tae him, but it scampers a bit away, movin really weird, archin its whole boady likesay. Magic wee silvery grey thing ... ken?
> Rents picks up a stane and flings it at the squirrel. Ah feel sick likes, ma hert misses a beat as it whizzes past the wee gadge. He goes tae pick up another, laughin like a maniac, but ah stoap um.
> – Leave it man. Squirrel's botherin nae cunt likesay! Ah hate it the wey Mark's intae hurtin animals ... it's wrong man. Ye cannae love yirsel if ye want tae hurt things like that ... ah mean ... what hope is thir? The squirrel's fuckin lovely. He's daein his ain thing. He's free. That's mibbe what Rents cannae stand. The squirrel's free, man.[3]

Spud's weirdness is apparent in his diction as well as his anti-social habits; but he articulates the key insight in the novel, and in so doing implies a depth of humanity with which the reader can identify. The outsider teaches us about ourselves. What of *Marabou Stork*?

Portraying the Strang family as a collection of emotional pathologies cohering around a shared name, the author does stop short of making them blind albinos plucking banjoes, and with a propensity for raping passing strangers. Well, he stops short of banjoes anyway. What do we learn of John Strang's inner life, other than that he's a mad bastard? We see Vet, his wife, from the outside, as Roy perceives her, figuring for him almost exclusively as a source of embarrassment. Located in Roy's mind, the narrative gives little room for anyone else's. From assorted ugly schemies to interchangeable ugly Afrikaaners, and the 'realness' of Strang's romance with Dorie in Manchester, cartoon substitutes for character, the cast is never other than 'other'. What we're left with, for too much of its content, is a kind of voyeurism, writing whose only major effect is to provoke outrage. Shock tactics in the context of *Trainspotting* are effective because they are funny, and many of them add to the human frailty portrayed; in its successor, less humour or pathos flatten the effect.

Other minor inconsistencies inhibit its success too. Strang occasionally translates his dialect into English; John Strang writes computer files in a transcribed version of his own accent, unlikely in someone unused to creative writing. And the odd anachronism creeps in (satellite dishes in the mid-1970s). *Marabou Stork Nightmares* is not as subtle, ironic or insightful as its predecessor, the reach of its ambition frequently exceeding its grasp of craft.

More importantly, some of the book's critics complain of its lack of moral responsibility, but, on the contrary, in offering an alternative perspective to that of its characters, the author arrays moral judgements at every turn. Among these are revelations of various right-wing prejudices, from John's pro-Thatcher/Britain rhetoric and the propaganda in the South African Museum (pp.81-2) to the Defence advocate in the Casuals' rape trial:

> I don't know who's put her up to this, some dykey feminist group trying to make the unfortunate wench into a *cause celebre*, no doubt. Well, she has two chances, slim and none. (p.207)

Or save-our-Health-Service asides, as when two nurses discuss the moving of Strang's bed into a corridor:

> – I think it's terrible though. Some rich private patient needs the room, so a long-term, coma victim is dumped in the corridor until the wealthy case is ready to go ...
> – The hospital needs the funds these people bring in though, Tricia. (p.39)

And Strang's moment of truth, when contemplating his anger against the bourgeois cunts from his work:

> It all came tae ays wi clarity; these are the cunts we should be hurtin, no the boys we knock fuck oot ay at the fitba, no the birds we fuck aboot, no oor ain Ma n Dad, oor ain neighbours, oor ain mates. These cunts. Bit naw; we terrorise oor ain people. (pp.200-1)

You don't say! As revelations go, this is pretty prosaic. Far from amorality, Welsh exemplifies in this way the most excruciating politically correct editorialising of his material, culminating in reference to the Zero Tolerance campaign. A cautionary tale, Roy Strang's recollection is too late to redeem him, but at least brings enlightenment to him. Like a late twentieth century Charles Dickens, Welsh offers his reader moral progress among urban squalor, his hero coming to maturity the postmodern way, David Copperfield with his dick in his mouth.

That a sting in the tail of the novel may be found in the potential unreliability of Roy will not have escaped notice. Perhaps, as David

Hume indicated in his Enlightened scepticism alluded to in the introductory epigraphs of the novel, Strang's account has no causal connection with the world beyond his subjective state; maybe he is merely expressing his self-loathing, through two layers of invented experience, in abstract and realist modes, entirely in his own head. In which case, did the rape really take place? Does Kirsty actually part him from his penis? If we believe Roy then we see his self-hate enacted for real in a fictional world; if we doubt him, then he dramatises his self-hate in his imagination only. Either way, Strang's Youth-in-Asia comes to pass; and we have a narrative inscribed with inferiorism, the Scot silencing himself. Like ah sais, not fuckin quoted. In this respect, the impetus of *Marabou Stork*, for all its innovation, is to polarise the lives it portrays into a barbaric 'other' status. Where *Trainspotting* sets up and then undermines its social and literary conventions with sophisticated, searching irony, the second novel only sets them up. The narrative stance is distant from the content of the story, and the novel seems to confirm the prejudices of the kind of bourgeois perspective it is intended to challenge. In older literary tropes the Scot could be trusted to put his foot in his mouth; with Welsh's *oeuvre* it's a different organ, same effect.

Perhaps the symptoms of self-loathing must inevitably stalk the literature of a fractured and dependent culture. Irvine Welsh has an extraordinary talent with which he can achieve great things; at a time of great diversity in writing, he has been celebrated for forging an authentic modern voice in Scottish fiction. But that voice may be in danger of perpetrating another kind of forgery, passing off received cultural stereotype as authenticity. As young authors follow Welsh's lead, portraying the under-class for the literate class appears to be as much an expression of the Scottish cultural cringe as a challenge to it. Not quite the legacy Burns intended: to see ourselves as 'others'. Fiction in Scotland has come a long way in a short time and Welsh is currently at its forefront; but maybe Cripple Creek is still in sight.

Notes
1. Irvine Welsh, *Marabou Stork Nightmares* (London: Jonathan Cape, 1995). All page references are to this edition.
2. Gavin Wallace, 'The Novel of Damaged Identity', *The Scottish Novel since the Seventies*, eds. Gavin Wallace and Randall Stevenson (Edinburgh University Press, 1993), pp. 217-231, p.220.
3. Irvine Welsh, *Trainspotting* (Secker & Warburg, 1993), p.159.

two poems

Ian Cadman

Fuck

Can you say fuck on the radio?
what? you can't use the F word
what fucking F word?
FUCK OFF
fucking stupid innit
can't say fuck? everyone says fuck
FUCK OFF
can't bring themselves to say fuck
so they have to fucking say
the fucking F word
FUCK OFF
fuck can mean fucking anything
fucking *brilliant* word fuck innit
FUCK OFF
d'you know why they don't like fuck?
because its about fucking sex innit
and its about fucking violence
FUCK OFF
fuck's a fucking link between
fucking sex and fucking aggression
fucking not nice for people
FUCK OFF
so we all fucking pretend
the worlds so fucking nice
well it isn't fucking nice
you fucking die for a fucking start
then you're fucking fucked aren't you
FUCK OFF
and we're all so fucked up
because you can't fucking say
fuck   in public
I mean that's what fucking Freud said

a hundred fucking years ago isn't it
he said we're all fucking ill
because no Fucker can be their fucking self
but we wouldn't be fucking here
if it wasn't for fucking so
FUCK OFF
It's more fucking dangerous
fucking pretending   I mean
it's your fucking instinct   innit
all men are Fuckers that's fucking right Mrs
I mean you can say fuck sometimes
like James fucking Kelman
four thousands fucks in a fucking book?
FUCK OFF
you can say fuck but you can't say cunt
can you?
but you can't have a fuck without a cunt
so that's even more fucking stupid
FUCK OFF
the whole fucking planets   fucking at it
the fucking birds the fucking bees
you can't keep that fucking fucking down
FUCK OFF
I want to be fucking alive
not fucking dead

Guidelines in Society

you see   society
just cannot function   unless
people behave in a certain way
within   certain guidelines

I'm *telling you*   WHAT?
if you put one foot wrong in
Tescos   or   ha   B&Q anywhere   normal
like that
we'll come down heavily   because
You Need Help

Now   tell me
do you ever feel as if you're
possessed by evil spirits?
da cdabzchan y arr   da cazavy arr

de orr vzze ga   caneearr   zee   yaaaahhhhh

because you see it's like this
normality is good   but
madness   is eeeeevil   a ha ha hahahahahaaa
you see it all goes back to the
Devil
on da cod y bod y   yaaah
  da chan dy   gid y   zya h   yaaahaaaa

we're needing an exorcist
exorcism   here   that's my diagnosis
but
all that possession business
that's all in the past now
everythings fine   now
no problem   at all
I mean   honestly   the pressure of modern life
can get too much for *some* people
it's the stress   you see
now we've got proper treatment
what we do is
we put on white coats
and put twenty thousand volts
through their head while
they're strapped down
that keeps them as right as rain
or if that doesn't work
we fill them up with tranquilizers
and that soon   gets them   back
to nooorrrmmaaaalll   like
e-v-e-r-y-o-n-e   e-l-s-e

normality
where everyone's nice and normal
everyones's nice and normal
normality
where no one   dies
well   you never have to see a
dead body   not these days
that's not normal
well we may have to lock you up
so *will you listen to sense   I mean*
just keep the head down   and
get on with the work

it's ok to be cheerful
it's ok to be happy

BUT DON'T GET ECSTATIC
THERE'S NO ROOM FOR ECSTASY IN SOCIETY

Oh please   restrict yourself haha
to being mediocre boring   and   dull
for everyones sake
if not your own

it's ok to get down
it's ok to   maybe   get
a little   depressed   it's only normal
but don't get
Suicidal
we can't have people
throwing themselves off buildings
oh no no no no   no
keep the head down
get on with the work   don't
even think about it
because if you did   think about it
you might   go
MAAAAAAAAAD
honestly if you *started* to think
about it
even for a minute
the way the world's going and
everything in it   well   ha
I mean if I thought about it
I'd probably kill myself
immediately
a ha ha hahahahahahahaaaaaa

Ian Cadman lives in Perth, Scotland. Sixteen of his poems were published in *Edinburgh Review* 78-79

> Afraid of madness, of going mad, we shun the word *mad*. We have created a huge battery of colloquialisms to poke fun at it, to show that we do not really care about it, and also a range of dispassionate technicalisms, the verbal equivalent of padded cells, to keep it under control ... ... when it come to madness, the path from euphemism to taboo is usually swift and straight.
>
> *Euphemisms*, John Ayto, London 1973

> ... In a barbarian society, we are forced to live in an asylum, where we are both patients and explorers. Certain rules, arrived at empirically, will govern our conduct in terms of that analogy.
>
> First, I recognise the seeds of madness in myself. I know that if ever, for any purpose, I allow myself to act as a member of such a [madhouse] group, I allow myself to forfeit my responsibility to my fellows, from that moment I am a madman, and the degree of my insanity will be purely fortuitous.
>
> Second I must suspect all bodies, groups, teams, gangs, based on power, for where two or three hundred are gathered together, there is the potentiality of lunacy in the midst of them, whether lunacy that kills Jews, lunacy that flogs Indians, lunacy that believes Lord George Gordon or the Ku Klux Klan, or lunacy that bombs Berlin. Yet I shall not hate or distrust any of my fellow patients singly. They are exactly as I am. I can see how dangerous they are, but I can be as dangerous to them if I allow myself to become involved. It will be said that I deny social responsibility. I do not – I believe that responsibility is boundless. We have boundless responsibility to every person we meet. The foreman owes it to his men not to persecute them – he owes it as a man, not because there is an abstract power vested in the TUC which demands it. Barbarism is a flight from responsibility, an attempt to exercise it towards a non-existent scarecrow rather than to real people. Each sincere citizen feels responsibility to society in the abstract, and none to the people he kills. The furious obedience of the Good Citizens is basically irresponsible.
>
> in *Writings Against Power and Death*, Alex Comfort, 1994

REVIEWS

The Autonomy of Modern Scotland
Lindsay Paterson
Edinburgh University Press, 1994

Revolving Culture
Angus Calder
I. B. Taurus, 1994

DAVID STENHOUSE

DURING the summer of 1988 I worked as a chaperon to a group of American High School students on an educational tour of Britain. As part of their stay in Edinburgh I took them to a talk by Alan Lawson, then the editor of *Radical Scotland* on the constitutional situation in Scotland. Lawson presented a detailed survey of Scotland's political status since 1707 and concluded by expounding the attractions of the SNP's policy of 'Independence in Europe'. Afterwards we all went on a more conventional tourist trail around Edinburgh, taking in Greyfriar's Bobby, the Castle and Calton Hill. Our guide was a Lothian Regional Transport Driver. Since the schoolkids were very excited by what they'd heard that morning, they asked the driver what his view of Scottish independence was. Driving around Calton Hill he replied 'Well, we've got our own legal system, our own type of schools and our own church. We might not be Independent but we are independent.' In *The Autonomy of Modern Scotland*, Lindsay Paterson expounds the driver's view.

Paterson starts with the premise that Unionists and Nationalists share a body of assumptions about what happened to Scotland in 1707, namely that Scotland gave up its Independence, and that control over Scotland has been exercised from London ever since. He then proceeds to ask why if Scotland has not 'been itself' for nearly 300 years, it is still distinctly 'itself' in a set of cultural assumptions and habitual activities. In order to pursue the answer to this question Paterson follows the meaning of 'autonomy' through various historical manifestations, from his model of 'a small nation choosing its fate in a constrained context [the Union]' in the 18th century up to the exercise of technocratic autonomy in the twentieth century:

> The bureaucracy was Scottish, through the Scottish Office which has grown to embrace most domestic policy. The pressure groups were Scottish, also increasingly so. The middle-class professions were at least as Scottish as the working-class one: accountancy, medicine, education, law enforcement, local-government administration and many others had professional bodies that were either wholly Scottish or else had an autonomous Scottish component. All of this was like a system of estates ... Scotland, indeed, came to be thought of as one large pressure group itself – an estate of the British realm – using its own bureaucracy to bargain for resources with London.

In addition to advancing this administrative model of autonomy, Paterson examines other small nations to see how they survived to the present day. He indicates that whereas the way in which Scotland survives may be unusual, the problems facing small countries tend to be similar, and others have dealt with those problems less well than Scotland. He concludes that for small nations autonomy was continually negotiated and compromised. Put in a nutshell, this section of the book argues that you are not necessarily without autonomy if you have no parliament, and neither are you guaranteed autonomy if you have a parliament.

Further, Paterson argues against the tendency to view the 18th or 19th centuries through the concerns of the 20th. He notes:

> at least since the nationalist cultural revival of the 1920s, the belief has gained currency that Scotland in the nineteenth century was subservient to England. This belief assumes that the only sure sign of not being subservient would have been a developed demand for an independent parliament.

One quibble with Paterson's view of the broad movement of Scottish Government would be why so many people involved in politics, and not just opposition politics either, but those with some experience of the workings of government have understood Scottish politics so very badly. Why, in short are there no spokespeople for the autonomy through technocracy position? It would seem to be a very good argument for leaving things the way they are, and as such of certain benefit to A Certain Party. In the absence of public spokespeople, Paterson's view of the split between the inside and outside of Scottish political life is deep and wide.

The Autonomy of Modern Scotland is not a book to make Paterson popular with those engaged in political activity on either side of the constitutional issue, but rather than a criticism, with many readers that is likely to be something of a recommendation. Despite its absolute reasonableness of tone this book is a profoundly subversive document.

Angus Calder's *Revolving Culture*, subtitled 'Notes From the Scottish Republic' is a collection of Reviews, Profiles and Review Articles which ranges from a survey of Scotland in the eighteenth century to an enquiry about Scottish Art at the end of the 1980s. Much of Calder's attractiveness as a writer lies in his style which, as Douglas Dunn notes in a cover quote 'crosses the barriers between academe and journalism'. In fact Calder seems to declare his own credo in 'Scotch Myths: The Patriot, The Manager and the Rebel' where he analyses the business of writing history:

> ... history without a modicum of 'artistic' flair and 'journalistic' persuasiveness is unreadable except by ultra specialists. Historians who have no strong convictions of any political or religious variety will be thereby stunted as human beings. The imagination which grasps the past must be nurtured by engagement in the present. No-one indifferent to feminist issues, for instance, is likely to seek and recover important new sources of understanding of women's history.

In addition to being an implicit statement of his own position, his essay is a fascinating study of the use which contemporary politicians, or those with a political axe to grind, make of Scottish history. So we have Paul Scott's Fletcher of Saltoun as a prophet of Independence in Europe and Michael Fry's Henry Dundas as a patriotic Scot who nevertheless threw in his lot with the forces of imperial 'progress'.

And if politicians have historical agendas then historians have political agendas. In 'Rewriting Scottish History' (which would have been just as good a title for the earlier essay) he exposes the assumptions of Rosalind Mitchison in *Lordship to Patronage: Scotland 1603-1745* as 'implicitly Unionist'. After she has regretted that Cromwell's conquest of Scotland was 'too short for major political benefits to be achieved' Calder interjects incredulously:

> Benefits? Under colonial rule? In six years of political unsettlement?

but he tempers this aside with the judgement that 'her account of the early eighteenth century transition from 'lordship' ... to 'patronage' ... looks durably convincing'. Nor is he politically biased; earlier he gives James D. Young with whom he might be in more agreement, a terrible review for the 'rambling, repetitious, unchronologised methods' on display in *John Maclean: Clydeside Socialist.*

Elsewhere too, Calder has an admirable knack for finding exactly the right phrase. He fingers Kenneth White for his wide eyed pilgrim act, and expresses a concern shared by many, though never so elegantly articulated, that 'this very clever man who deliberately denies himself recourse to irony, is performing an exquisite con-trick.'

The problem I have with this book is not that its individual elements aren't fine (most of them are brilliant), just that it doesn't hang together. Calder's strength is his ingenuity and sensitivity to what a writer is 'about', and in order to carry off that fine blend of sympathy and criticism he has to move close to his subjects. Because *Revolving Culture* shows him covering an extraordinary range of topics, the book doesn't have a single determining 'personality'. No-one wants to see where a writer is coming from all the time, but some predictability is needed to make a collection of articles into a book.

Taken together, these two books with their insistence that Scotland has real cultural (Calder) and administrative (Paterson) autonomy in its present constitutional situation might seem to echo Michael Foot's famous jibe to David Steel that he had passed from rising star to elder statesmen without passing through the intervening period of power. I wonder though if we're seeing an interesting new phase in the Scottish political/cultural debate. Since MacDiarmid defined Scottishness as a state of waiting-to-become, the arguments of Lindsay Paterson and the examples provided by Angus Calder suggest that statements about 'cultural independence' aren't just a good bit of rhetorical cheek; they might be the hallmarks of politics after the end of the MacDiarmid project. Like it or not we've entered the era of Post-Scottish Scottish politics.

A History Maker
Alasdair Gray
Canongate Press
ISBN 0 86241 495 4 £13.99

BERTHOLD SCHOENE

ALASDAIR Gray's latest novel, *A History Maker*, introduces us to a posthistoric age in which humankind has shrugged off the trammelling onuses of economic deprivation, political strife and marital coupledom, in which the vestigial remnants of old atomic power stations function as archaeological landmarks, and the majority of people live in small self-subsistent matriarchal family units gathered around all-providing powerplants. In such an edenic idyll there is absolutely no need for anyone to conform. People can drop out and choose to go to the stars, join the intergalactic species of *neosapiences* and become, like them, immortal. Or they can make the whole of Planet Earth their home and live as communally independent gangrels. Yet even in this world of ultimate personal freedom there is no universal sense of happiness. And if there were, there would probably be no tale to tell because stories do not exactly flourish in a utopian vacuum of eternal bliss.

Ingeniously, if paradoxically, Gray's plot derives its narrative impulse from the festering dynamics of posthistoric boredom, and male posthistoric boredom in particular. Warfare has become the major male pastime. Though fought to the death, the battle between the Ettrick clan and Northumbria United, which opens the main section of the novel, has about the meaningfulness and societal import of a football match, complete with sports reporters, an umpire and 'the bell for end of play'. In Gray's brave new world, the media are omnipresent as saucer-shaped 'public eyes', hovering above the battlefield like huge carrion flies to take in 'a picture to be replayed in slow motion for centuries to come' or spinning up unexpectedly from behind blueberry bushes to interview a startled VIP. A battle is considered a great success when it is likely to 'be disked by millions', with the slaughter of soldiers being 'viewed and viewed again to the last days of mankind and television and time'. Journalistic integrity and critical detachment have been replaced by the expedient imperative to pander to a gluttonous public voyeurism, a feature which Gray's dystopia shares with many postmodern cinematic creations like, for example, Quentin Tarantino's experiments or *Natural Born Killers* by Oliver Stone.

Wat Dryhope, Gray's hero, is the epitome of male boredom and discontent. His craving for history, 'a period of excitement when folk thought they were making a better world', alerts us to the fact that life within a perfect idyllic still outside the contingent turbulence of historical flux, is essentially inimical to the ambitious human spirit on its quest for self-fulfilment. His resentment of the matriarchal power structures that inform the world in which he lives, and his longing for a world in which 'men and women earn their living room by working together as equals' are not so much indicative of Wat's latent misogyny as of the extremely sexist nature of 23rd-century society. Women's liberation has clearly overshot its mark, perpetuating an insalubrious system based on a mutual exclusion and communal segregation of the sexes which ascribes major social significance to what are, as we all know, relatively minor biological differences. An eventual male rebellion against female omnicompetence and power seems pre-programmed. Hence, for example, Wat's desperate and uncharacteristically unreasonable outburst to his teenage lover Annie who, as a female, is his natural superior: 'I want the bad old days when wars had no rules and bombs fell on houses and men and women died together like *real* equals! Equal in agony and mutilation!'

As Wat's mother Kate suggests in her 'Notes & Glossary Explaining Obscurities', which make up roughly a fourth of the novel and turn out to constitute its meta-historical backbone, 'even loving families bred people who could only bear life by changing their world or finding another.' Two such people are her son Wat and her daughter Meg Mountbenger alias sexy Delilah to whose witch-like puddock call Wat, a 23rd-century Macbeth, succumbs one night on a lonely mountain path. Delilah, crazed by an unrequited baby love for her brother as well as the consequences of a premature rejuvenation process, that has succeeded in rendering her immortal yet left her emotionally unstable, is plotting to cause havoc in Utopia. She infects Wat with a virus apt to plague the world back into the twentieth century, killing off the powerplants and infecting all men with sudden military enthusiasm and nationalistic pathos. Luckily, the first ominous epicentric quakes of the potential disaster are registered and nipped in the bud by the great-grannies of Ettrick, whose 'gossip has been the only government and police the world has needed for more than a century.' The dull indigenous nightmare of a new national Scotland has been successfully pre-empted. Once again Gray frustrates the fallacious desire of old-fashioned Scottish literary critics to see Scottishness – that is, a closed catalogue of fixed values and typical characteristics, firmly rooted in a bedrock of anti-English sentiments – revived in Scottish literature. Instead, Gray concerns himself with more cosmopolitan matters, not an outdated feudist insistence on national difference but the vision of a truly utopian future emanating from a perfect gender equilibrium between interdependent men and women. Gray adumbrates this vision but does not care to elaborate on it, complying in great self-mocking irony with Kate Dryhope's historical observation that 'postmoderns had no interest in the future, which they expected to be an amusing rearrangement of things they already knew.'

a kamikaze in her eyes
peter plate
San Francisco: Pressure Drop Press, 1994
ISBN 0 9627091 4 X $10

BERTHOLD SCHOENE

QUITE in vain does one search for indices of a deliberate, artistically meaningful design or concept behind the awkward and highly amateurish prose style of peter plate's fourth novel, *a kamikaze in her eyes*. Clearly, its idiosyncratic layout has nothing to do with a concretist postmodern questioning of the nature of textuality but is merely self-indulgent gimmick. The author's style is that of a pulp novelist specialising in sour kitsch that flaunts its few corny (and horny) moments. In the course of the novel we are treated to some truly earth-shattering insights informing us, for example, that 'a divorce always made you feel like the past shared with a man was just a dream', or that 'the truth was poison; it caused pain.' Characters tear at their hair, turn green, gnash their teeth in frustration, duck behind living-room couches 'with the reflexes of a hunted animal', or look a hundred years old. In plate's novel people do not communicate or converse; instead, stilted passages of dialogue inundate the reader with a thesaurian plethora of synonymous inadequacies, causing dim silhouettes of soap-operatic stock to bark, bellow, blurt, bubble, croak, deadpan, drawl, enthuse, exult, groan, growl, grumble, grunt, hiss, intone, moan, mutter, pant, pout, rant, rasp, sigh, snap, snarl, sniff, snort, sob, sputter, whine and yell at one another. To our relief, no one ever 'ejaculates' which, however, is hardly surprising, considering the quality of the entirely gratuitous erotic sequences, of which there are plenty, detailing that 'she started to show him a few movements designed to improve his thrusting technique', that 'every time he had an orgasm, he died' and – not enough – that 'to her delight, his tongue was as long and as wide as the sole of a shoe. It was soft like a puppy dog's ear.'

plate's writing is that of someone imaginatively challenged. His imagery is a twisted coil of *non sequiturs*, violently incongruent and often verging on the grotesque – to no apparent effect. What are we, for example, supposed to make of descriptions like: 'Travelling had done something to her vocal cords, enriching them with dust and wind, and maybe a cigarette or two'; or: 'The sun looked like a flashlight positioned in between a flock of clouds. There was a chill in the air, but it was no worse than the cramp in her leg'? And when the red blinking lights of a video camera are likened to the eyes of rats, the extra information that it is 'the kind of rats that lived on farms somewhere in the country' is, honestly, fairly irrelevant. Also, can someone please tell the author that sharks are not known to 'nibble' on their victims and sparrows don't have 'talons' (unless, that is, they are of the predatory Steven Spielberg make)?

After almost choking on the novel's trite clichés and struggling to make sense of its unabashed inconsistencies, with daughters changing into sons and scornful pity growing into passionate love over a couple of pages, one still has the banalities of the plot to contend with. The promotional blurb promises us a compelling investigation of the difficult issue of euthanasia, an analysis of contemporary American family life as well as the psychological outline of two sexual awakenings, one male and heterosexual, the other female and lesbian. What we get instead are twenty-five badly written chapters filled to the brim with vacuous sensationalism and bathetic nonsense. plate's use of the subject of euthanasia is neither clever nor fervent, climaxing in ludicrous psychological portrayals like that of Micky, the doctor's mistress: 'But Micky didn't like to think about death. It disturbed her, like when she wanted to brush her teeth, but found the toothpaste tube had been squeezed dry. That emptiness, it was highly oppressive, always giving her an unrelenting headache.' The coming out as lesbian of the doctor's ex-wife, on the other hand, is described in terms of a post-marital, mid-life whim, involving no problematic identity crisis but happening just like that: 'After a while, Jay decided she was tired of cooking dinner for the three of them. The kids could feed themselves television dinners for all she cared. She started going out to a local women's bar. Her attraction to women was becoming important. It was new, and because she was having fun, it was entirely foreign.' Not one of the characters in the novel ever starts his or her own life; all of them remain confined to their wordy origin in the author's imagination. Unsurprisingly, plate does not grant lesbian women their own sexual aesthetics. Jay's salacious ogling of the anorexic news reporter Zela is firmly rooted in a straight male obsession with legs, breasts and 'precious ankles'.

The Facts of Life: the Creation of Sexual Knowledge in Britain, 1650–1950
Roy Porter and Lesley Hall
Yale University Press, ISBN
£19.95

MARIO RELICH

'WE are in almost total ignorance of the personal sexual beliefs and behaviour of all but the tiniest minority in the world we have lost.' Such a declaration reveals that Roy Porter and Lesley Hall are not easily deluded as medical historians, but their book also points to the chink of light in the darkness. It consists of the fact that sexual advice literature provides important clues about the sexual beliefs of our ancestors.

Porter covers 'the long 18th century', and Hall writes about the Victorian period and after, both very much concerned with the 'underlying politics of sexual knowledge' in sexual advice literature. One of the most influential books of the period, according to Porter, was by the French physician Nicolas Venette. His book was initially translated as *The Mysteries of Conjugal Love Reveal'd* (1703), and it was popular throughout the 18th century and beyond, becoming *Conjugal Love, or The Pleasures of the Marriage Bed* by 1774. Porter demonstrates that Venette's 'frame of reference was quintessentially physical', and it was overwhelmingly so with sexual advice books of the time. Venette, however, also focused on how the conflicting dictates of love and sex can be harmonized within marriage. For the French doctor, in fact, sex and love were relatively straightforward matters which could be settled simply by getting married first, and then 'following Nature'.

By the latter part of the 18th century, more attention began to be paid to the psychological aspects of sexuality, and this was reflected in the cult of sensibility. As Porter puts it: 'Sexual attraction found expression in an aesthetic, elevated language, brimful of feeling. Tenderness was underlined by the growing delicacy of the language employed.' Boswell was a good example of such delicacy. He would ask a woman he fancied: 'How then can I be happy? What time?'

Paradoxically, however, the emphasis on feeling and psychological factors, not to mention 'the pursuit of happiness', paved the way for the therapeutic quackery of a physician like James Graham. His 'Celestial Bed' was rented out to infertile couples at £50.00 a time, complete with soft music, mirrors and other enticements. Like Venette, he set great store by moderate sexual pleasures within marriage, but unlike him was also one of the first to warn against masturbation. Porter cannot resist the following deflating summing-up of the society doctor's career: 'Follow my advice and live to 150, boasted the man who died at 49.'

Porter's style is often brisk and humorous, while Hall's is more understated, often adopting the tone of a sceptical feminist. Her analysis of an unpublished 'Report on Sex' survey from *Mass Observation* in the late 1940s is particularly sardonic. She reveals that an 'outstanding discovery' by the middle-class interviewers was, to quote from one of them, 'the contrast between our initial expectation of inhibition, embarrassment and rebuff – and the friendly and cooperative manner with which our questions were answered.'

As Hall points out, the Victorians, far from being reticent about sex and sexuality, witnessed an explosion of sexual advice books. It is true that many of these focused grimly on venereal disease, and the perils of what was euphemistically called 'self-abuse'. But at least later on in Victoria's reign 'sexology' also flourished. Prominent sexologists included Havelock Ellis, Edward Carpenter and, as co-author with J. Arthur Thomson, of *The Evolution of Sex* (1889), and *Sex* (1914), Patrick Geddes.

The sexologists tended to be radical in their 'Whiggish enthusiasm for sexual liberation', prone to utopian ideals, and questioned assumptions about the subordination of women. They were also prepared to countenance the varieties of sexual experience. Carpenter, for instance, wrote *The Intermediate Sex* (1908). It is, however, with *Married Love* (1918), by Marie Stopes, which dared to discuss sexual techniques, and not just for procreation, that the modern sexual advice book really emerges. It was a bestseller, even if Stopes was reviled by some, like the sexologists before her, but Hall finds her selection of letters about sexual matters from working-class women, *Mother England* (1929), just as significant. Its subtitle, 'A Contemporary History self-written by those who have no historian', anticipates much 'history from below' today.

Although Porter and Hall treat sexuality as a form of discourse, much like Foucault did, they take issue with his absurd claim that the Victorians were no more sexually repressed than we are. Sexuality, until *very* recently, as Porter points out, ' ... was a domain of life that was furtive and shameful, as was the body itself, whose fragmented past is only now being pieced together.' *The Facts of Life*, with illustrations to match, reads like an essential contribution to such an endeavour.

Bunker Man
Duncan McLean
Jonathan Cape, 1995
ISBN 0 224 04154 1 £9.99 p/b

R. A. JAMIESON

THE OLD MAXIM 'Never judge a book by its cover' is generally good advice, but there are some book covers which illustrate their contents perfectly. So it is with Duncan McLean's second novel. Gunnie Moberg's atmospheric cover photo shows exactly what you get – the off-centre view from deep in the bunker, a parka-clad figure framed in the tiny doorway, hood zipped up to hide the face. Oppressive darkness inside, and indefinable strangeness at the door.

Bunker Man is a story in which doors figure prominently. It is the tale of Robert Catto, a supposedly superfit 30 year old who recently moved to his new wife Karen's home town on the northeast coast of Scotland, where he has been employed as head janitor at the local secondary school. In the opening scene, Rob is woken in the night by Karen, who thinks she hears someone moving around in their house. Though nothing but an unlocked back door is discovered, this incident introduces the idea of the intruder, and a mysterious 'lurker' – probably a recipient of what the Tory government euphemistically call Community Care – is later seen hanging around the school grounds.

At first the newly weds seem well balanced, fond of yet not obsessed by sex, but soon there are signs that Rob resents his partner's higher social status – and salary – working for an oil company. Then, on a trip together to one of her childhood's secret shoreline places, Karen loses her keys in an alfresco romp and when he goes back to search for them, Rob, seeking shelter from the rain, stumbles on the lurker's hideaway: this stranger has made his base in a World War II defence on the coastline near the school environs, a bunker used only by those townsfolk who have something to hide. In a small alcove there, Rob finds the missing keys.

The mystery deepens. By settling in the bunker, the stranger unwittingly associates himself in Catto's mind with the drug-taking, illicit sex and under-age drinking that the bunker plays host to – the very evils that Rob's job demands he must oppose. Yet the relation between the two characters is akin to that of doppelganger. Although both are outsiders in the town, one has been welcomed into a position of responsibility and inhabits the daylight, while the other apparently sneaks through the shadows, spying on folk. The irony is that Rob's social function is partly that of spy, keeping a lookout for the lurker, supervising the pupils and the other janitors. So the image of the stranger plagues the increasingly paranoid Rob, who goes running in order to blank his mind:

> What tended to happen was that a thought came into his head, and he'd start to follow it, but before very long there'd be a big thump and the thought would get knocked clean away. The thump was his foot hitting the ground. A couple of seconds later the same thought might appear again, or a new one crop up, but no matter what they were they only ever stuck in his skull for half a moment till his trainer hit the tarmac and they got jolted out. [p. 25]

But the thoughts come whatever, and before long Rob's suspicions have turned him into a peeper, looking for evidence of his wife's adultery. In fact Rob is not only the finder-keeper of the keys, but the master of the keyholes. The erotic symbolism in this is important – and of course the doorkeeper knows what is hidden on the other side. Catto's ambivalent place on the threshold between corrupted tradition and contemporary protocol is cleverly illustrated in a scene where he goads his father-in-law into an Alf Garnett-like statement of pre-PC commonplaces of racist prejudice. Later, to Karen, Catto claims not to share these views although he is obviously privy to them and acquiescent of their right to exist:

> You know me Karen, he said. You know the score. You don't have to be black to be a cunt, I know that. I mean look at the fucking playground pervert, he's not black. But he is a cunt. He's a weirdo... ...Your dad blames blacks for all the ills of the world, but I know it's not their fault. It's the sick bastards who're to blame, the weird cunts, the cunts in hoods on sunny days. [p. 180]

By this stage these words are likely to conjure the image of a jogger with hood up as readily as the mysterious stranger in parka, because the novel has already turned on the emergence of another character into the story: a fourteen year-old pupil, Sandra Burnett. Catto first encounters her as the source of some pornographic magazines circulating in school, which she has pinched from under her father's bed. She is a slovenly Lolita, remarkable for little bar her diffidence, but the descriptions of Rob's sex life which have previously hinted vaguely at perversion begin then to grow in significance. His fumbled attempts at saving Sandra 'from herself' end with sex in a school cupboard. Sandra is the pliable object Rob requires to play out his fantasies, in contrast to his wife Karen who satisfies his desire for social status and respectability. Sandra's sketchily related messed-up life, which consists largely of sensation mistaken for love, makes her the perfect victim for Catto's repressed sadistic nature.

Once their affair is begun, the threshold between the two male characters is crossed. Catto becomes the 'Bad Man', the corrupter of young lives, but can only admit to this in his hornytalk to Sandra. For his abuse of her to be made public would destroy everything he still struggles to protect, so he projects all his own guilt onto the figure of the stranger, the eponymous 'bunker man'. Catto tracks him down and befriends him. He is able to control the simple-minded outsider as easily as he can Sandra. The narrative races towards a melodramatic conclusion, in which Rob's plan to punish those he has designated as the wrong-doers and elevate himself again in his wife's estimation with a single stroke so nearly works out. The heavy-handed final scene makes it plain that he and the stranger have changed positions – Catto has become the voyeur, the bunker man, literally, the fucker.

Symbolically, *Bunker Man* seems to suggest that the traditionally dominant aggressive male, under severe pressure from the advance of women's liberation evidenced by Karen's social superiority, is robbed of the role of protector and provider, and pushed beyond the edge of civilised society. He is metaphorically in the bunker, under fire – and responds aggressively. This is underlined in the scene where Rob pays a call on Karen's older womanfriend. Susan, a divorcee of independent mind, but according to Rob an 'old slag', is loosely associated with the shadowy figure of the lurker because of a mysterious incident early in the novel when the bunker man interrupts a birthday meal in a restaurant by calling Susan to the door, claiming that he knows her.

Like Rob and the bunker man, Susan is a watcher, but she is a parent where the others are not. Above *her* door is the motto of the Lighthouse Board – IN SALUTEM OMNIUM – 'for the safety of all' – and in her window, a brass telescope. What Susan sees is that Rob is abusing her friend's love, although at first she attempts friendly reconciliation. Rob rejects this and Susan lets slip that she had advised Karen 'not to throw herself away' on Rob five years before, and that she hasn't changed her opinion since. She makes it clear that in her opinion he has no useful role in Karen's life. Under threat, Catto's response is to go, quite literally, on the offensive:

> If I hear of you putting ideas into my wife's head, I'm going to come round here, I'm going to get the big brass telescope from the window and I'm going to jam it up your cunt. Then I'll have a good look around, to see what signals you're showing, see how you like having *your* life poked about at. [p. 238]

By this point in the novel, the sexual act of penetration has become a twisted yearning to get inside the female, to look deep within even if it causes the woman pain, and it recurs in another scene near the end of the story when, concealed in one of the school's hideaways, Rob inserts a pencil torch inside his fourteen year old sex-slave's vagina in the declared hope of seeing what women are really like on the inside. This ridiculously wrong-headed idea stands metonymic for the nature of the madness Catto has retreated into. It is as if he wants to somehow get back inside the female, the womb, the maternal embrace. Denied this, he bursts with aggressive frustration into attacking what he loves:

> ...He shot out his arm and caught her round the waist.
> Let me go.
> I want to talk to you.
> I don't want to talk to you, you bastard.
> Karen, Karen ... He put his other arm around her too, and tried to bring her close to him, but she leant back and pushed her hands against his chest. Karen, I just want a bosie.
> Let me go!
> Look, he said, and squeezed tight with his arms, Stop fighting or they'll think I'm fucking attacking you. [p. 179]

'Bosie', a North East Scots word for 'bosom' is also, according to the Concise Scots Dictionary, 16th Lallans for 'womb', and Rob's avowed disgust at of those things outwith convention, like 'those cunts who wear hoods on sunny days', is perhaps perverted desire for the taboo of the mother – what starts as a deep need for a loving embrace turns into abuse.

But there are bosies and there are bosies. Sandra is under-age and unchallenging, Susan is over-age and all too challenging. Both are, from the perspective of the town's social convention, illicit. Only Karen's bosie is safe and sanctioned – as the bunkers of home and the janitor's 'bothy' are in comparison with the old wartime fortification. For ultimately, bunkers and bosies both represent the safe place and the bunker of the title itself, a womb-like structure with a single narrow entrance, is perhaps some kind of neglected Oedipal retreat, which in Rob's mind the outsider has no right to claim as his home.

Interestingly, the defence of the safe place against intruders is also a recurrent theme, in the actions and the fantasies of both the 'bunker man' and the 'bad man' – as the 'bunker man' seeks to protect his safe place in his war against the flocks of seabirds that surround his 'home', so Catto sees himself defending the safety of school and house against the threat of the 'lurker', the perversion and drug abuse Catto believes him to be guilty of spreading. Yet the pathetic figure of the bunker man hardly seems any more capable of such action than the seagulls are of destroying the bunker. The implication is that in Catto's paranoid culture of the masculine, boys – once they are turned out of the womb – are meant for war, and where no actual threat exists, one must be invented in order for them to have a function to perform, with madness and/or badness the outcome. But the war isn't against nation, class against class, race against race any longer – it's a desperate one against one, every man for himself struggle and survival is the prize, as he explains to Karen:

> ...every man is an enemy of every other man, a competitor, a rival. We all hate each other. You can't relax for a second for fear of getting stabbed in the back. That's what being a man's like. Not much wonder I'm jealous of this thing you women have – this trust and helping each other. [p. 231]

As a portrayal of a man losing all control over his thoughts and actions, *Bunker Man* is compelling, and Rob Catto is memorable as one of contemporary Scottish fiction's most despicable creations. There is a parallel with Hogg's *Private Memoirs and Confessions of a Justified Sinner* in that Catto, as a member of the town's elect, believes himself justified in punishing any supposedly dangerous deviant, but whereas Hogg's novel is an intricate weaving of very different narratives which seems to pre-empt many of the concerns of postmodernism, *Bunker Man* is a single thread, like Robert Wringhim's story without an 'Editor's Narrative' to contextualise it. Consequently, although Catto's breakdown is convincing, the reasons for it remain obscure. Although the evil-doer is ultimately exposed when the spy is himself spied in the final scene, the viewpoint is consistently that of the disturbed male and there is no narratorial analysis to bring the shocking conclusion into focus.

Similarly, bearing in mind recent understanding of how often sexual abuse is a kind of disease transmitted from victim to victim, generation by generation, it might be thought surprising that Catto's background goes largely unexplored. The restrictive nature of McLean's present-time consciousness narration allows only the barest revelation of his characters' pasts, and it could be argued that a narrative which unfolds scene after scene in strict chronological order with only slight reference of the fictional present to events preceding the timeframe of the dramatic storyline is unsuitable to the difficult and convoluted subject matter of *Bunker Man* – leaving the reader with the afterthought that one of the keys on the doorkeeper's ring might usefully have unlocked the door to the past.

Yet the result is a powerful psychological thriller which disturbs as much by means of its eschewal of psychology as by the details of the dark tale told – and maybe this the crux of McLean's method. Instead of explication of how the past shapes Catto, *Bunker Man* is a deliberately obscured view, necessary to create that sense of 90's man detached from but longing for the certainties of the past – the imperial mother culture. Hunkered down in a derelict bunker, he is desperately seeking the right key to lock the contemporary world out, unaware that the outside door is no longer there. To explain would be to mediate the terror of the unknown, and so remove the mood of random occurrence that is central to the novel's power.

As with the front cover, through the narrow opening of McLean's fictional method, the figure of a mysterious hooded man can be seen, ominously filling the doorframe – but by the time the book is closed, the reader knows that the real enemy is on the inside, that the cover view is Rob's, that he is the real bunkered man, a dangerous and frightened animal cowering in the immense darkness of his own warped prejudice. Despite its horror-genre ending, *Bunker Man* is a courageous exposition of the darkest depths that a man can fall to when cultured in the oppositions of gender, race and class struggle.

John Duncan: A Scottish Symbolist
John Kemplay
Pomegranate Artbooks, 1994
ISBN 1 55640 991 8 £20

MURDO MACDONALD

THE interest developing in the real achievements, rather than the imaginary failures, of the Celtic Revival in the Scotland of the late nineteenth and early twentieth century is given further impetus by the publication of the first book on the painter John Duncan (1866-1945). John Kemplay has already helped to illuminate the art of this period in his book on Cecile Walton and Eric Robertson, both of whom were followers of Duncan. This title immediately and appropriately situates Duncan in a tradition which includes the Pre-Raphaelites and French painters such as Pierre Puvis de Chavannes (1824-98).

Like these artists, Duncan saw painting as essentially an illustrative and decorative endeavour. He rejected the quasi-scientific analyses of 'reality' put forward by the impressionists in favour of a model of art which draws directly on earlier, more spiritually focussed, notions of art. The two main currents he drew on were Celtic art of the eight and ninth centuries, and the art of the early Italian Renaissance. His work can be regarded as an attempt to fuse these two influences into one whole.

Along with his older Edinburgh contemporary Phoebe Traquair, he believed that the unity of spirit and craft that can be seen in these earlier periods must be at the heart of any true art. With respect to Italian art, this ideology was to prove double-edged for Duncan, in turn inspiring him to remarkable work, and holding up the completion of that work through an obsession with experiments in the composition of tempera paint. Tempera was the favoured medium of the Italians of the fourteenth and fifteenth centuries, but whatever formulation Duncan was using he always seemed to think that something was missing. This aspect of Duncan is brought out well by John Kemplay, and it gives a fascinating insight into the painter's personality.

Another value of Kemplay's book is that he draws attention to the significance of Duncan's relationship with one of the main advocates of the Celtic Revival in Edinburgh, Patrick Geddes. Refering to the year 1891 when Duncan returned from Paris to his home town of Dundee, Kemplay says: 'As events turned out, he was destined not to be a portrait painter, and it is certain that his imminent meeting with the botanist and sociologist Patrick Geddes [then Professor of Botany at University College, Dundee] was the reason for his moving into a more creative phase as a painter. There can be little doubt that Geddes rearranged Duncan's outlook on art in order to help Geddes proceed along the highway of sociological reform, leaving Duncan to follow a byway of art from which he was unable to escape. The effect Geddes had on Duncan cannot be overstressed; in Duncan, Geddes found a sympathetic listener to his views on art, and no doubt Duncan was impressed by the undertakings Geddes had in mind.' This is fair comment. It was this association with Geddes that gave Duncan the unique place he holds in the history of Scottish art and ideas. Kemplay perhaps does not explore this as much as he might, because he is approaching Duncan primarily as a painter rather than as a graphic artist. While, from a broad perspective, one could consider this as a weakness in the book, it is more important to treat Kemplay's work as a significant starting point for the study of Duncan.

There is a great deal that Kemplay says which sheds light on the links between Duncan and Geddes, not least with respect to Duncan's close involvement with Geddes's Summer Meetings in the 1890s, and his leadership of Geddes's fruitful but short-lived Old Edinburgh School of Art. The latter was a key source of Celtic revival ornamental ideas, and it was artists – including Robert Burns, Helen Hay, Charles Mackie and Nellie Baxter – working with Duncan who provided the art for Patrick Geddes's extraordinary magazine *The Evergreen*. What is interesting here is that despite disappointments and uncertainties, Duncan stuck with Geddes's ideas of the significance of traditional, usually Celtic, culture in a modern context for the rest of his life. Here Kemplay's book becomes a valuable visual resource. The reader can move easily from early directly-Geddes related illustrative oil paintings such as *Jehanne d'Arc et sa Garde Ecossaise*, from 1896, and *The Taking of Excalibur* from the following year, to Duncan's fine evocations of Celtic and Christian-Celtic myth in his chosen medium of tempera such as *The Riders of the Sidhe*, 1911, *Tristan and Iseult*, 1912, *St Bride*, 1913, and *The Adoration of the Magi*, 1915.

Later still, in works such as *A Masque of Love* from 1921 – which shows a procession of lovers including Orpheus, Semele, Psyche, Sappho, St Francis, Perceval, Tristan and Iseult – one sees Duncan giving visual expression to Geddes's ideas of comparative mythology.

Cosmopolitan Greetings
Allen Ginsberg
Penguin Poets 1994
ISBN 0140587365 £7.99 pb

MATT EWART

GINSBERG appeared twice in Glasgow during the hot summer of 1973, singing/reading from memory, droning liltingly on a squeeze-box, insisting joyfully that love, openness of heart, were the only way to 'first thought, best thought'. On each occasion at the Arts Council building, Blythswood Square around 100 people, some in suits (councillors, curious bankers, company directors, people from church), mostly in light/bright colours, or in white linen/cheesecloth – cheesecloth! – tapped feet, smiled, swayed to a rhythmic poetic gamut of homosexual celebration, mysticism, politics and instantaneous inspirational word-play. Here was an artist/guru/teacher at one with his work, and immediately at one with us.

This collection of recent 'greetings' – what else could they be – is Ginsberg's first since the marvellous *White Shroud* in 1986, and contains that same sense/mix of spontaneity and important message, adding once more to that essential Ginsberg continuity that speaks of self as person *and* messenger through change in time, yet not in world:

> Will another hundred thousand desert deaths across the world be cause for the next rejoicing?
> *After the Big Parade* (p68)

This is poetry as drum-beat reportage and commentary, using poetry as means (and end) to that understanding of a world both flawed and beautiful. There is process at work in everything – the emphasis is on finding the right process, since for Ginsberg the secret processes of the world and of poetry are ultimately – crucially – to be sought out and unified:

> The psychiatrist said
> "If you're going to talk to yourself,
> do it in the form of poetry".
> *John* (p73)

Just the same, if there's a flaw in this book, bringing an irony to the word 'greetings', it may be in a kind of gathering darkness, a sadness brought about by ageing, and a sense of having seen so much. Ginsberg is now 69, with security and recognition as a member of the American Academy of Arts and Letters, and a recipient in 1993 of the medal of Chevalier d'Ordre des Arts et Lettres by the French Minister of Culture. This is the same man whose iconoclastic energies in 1965 had him simultaneously expelled from Communist Prague and placed on the FBI's Dangerous Security List. Perhaps such events now prompt doubt, dismay:

> If I had a spirit I forgot
>   when I was breathing
> If I had a speech it was
>   all a boast
> If I had a desire it went
>   out my anus
> *After Lalon* (p77)

Then again, what poet has not written of doubt, even converted it to a kind of challenge? It can be the other side of exuberant proclamation – 'I am the King of May' – that has always been Ginsberg's certain strength. There may be, also, warnings for all of us in these words, for it has been Ginsberg's calling also to warn:

> Ginsberg says Gog and Magog Armageddon did the job
> *Hum Bom* (p66)

Let's look closely at the key words used in the above quoted portion of 'After Lalon'. These are 'spirit', 'breathing', 'speech', 'boast', 'anus'. We can be reminded in the last word of Ginsberg's homosexuality, but also of defiance. Similarly, going backwards along the word-list, 'boast' holds the warning of egoism, but also suggests defiance, challenge. This is echoed in much of Ginsberg's poetry, and we can imagine the message: 'You are the materialist capitalist heterosexuals, claiming love, pleasure, boasting of success, but that is no success.' Yet it is in the words 'speech', 'breathing', 'spirit' that, surely, we are reminded of the essence of Ginsberg's poetic, and religious, search and meaning. It is in Buddhism that Ginsberg finds unity in these three terms, and finds the unifying force for his life and his work:

> I write poetry because my mind wanders subject to sex politics Buddhadharma meditation
> *Improvisation in Beijing* (Preface)

From the same poem:

> I write poetry because the English word Inspiration comes from Latin Spiritus, breath, I want to breathe freely

In Buddhism breath is sacred, and is part of the Cosmic Breath. Spirit is expressed through the right breathing producing the right speech. Poetry, rhythmic sound, is the sound of the spirit breathing.

> All gone all gone all overgone now all gone sky-high
> old mind so Ah!
> *Return of Kral Majales* (p42)

Ginsberg may be a member of the American Academy, but he is also co-founder of the Jack Kerouac School of Disembodied Poetics, the first accredited western Buddist college, where poetry is an essential teaching. There it is studied what it means to say 'first thought, best thought', and announce 'I'm going to try speaking some reckless words, and I want you to try to listen recklessly'.

Ginsberg's recklessly endless polemic against political oppression and its seed-source, cultural oppression, inspires for him its corollary, Buddhist compassion:

> Return return reborn in spirit and knowledge in human body my own or others as continual Teacher of chaotic peace
> *Supplication for the Rebirth of the Vidyadara* (p67)

It has been Ginsberg's purpose, ever since the 1950s Beat Generation and the publication of *Howl*, to synthesise into a future/ancient Western/Eastern Mind the apparently disparate, yet powerful, human energies at large in the world – energies often destructive, yet with vast potential. This is no job for a poet, we may say, still often stuck with notions of poetry as a kind of grace and favour romance. But Ginsberg puts his life and his soul on the line for a much larger meaning, put simply in

'Proclamation': In any case you can believe every word I say'. We should return the 'greetings' of this disturbingly beautiful collection and do just that.

Political Landscape
Martin Warnke (trans. David McLintock)
Reaktion Books, 1994
ISBN 0 948462 63 9 £12.95

JIM LAWSON

Martin Warnke's book, *Political Landscape*, consists of six chapters; or rather they are six essays, or perhaps even lectures, accompanied by copious illustration. It is published in the series *Essays in Art and Culture* and therefore stands in distinquished company alongside works by Roger Cardinal and Norman Bryson, among others.

The title announces the limitations within which the text intends to function. There will be no aesthetic landscape, nor moral landscape or social landscape or classical landscape. But the subtitle announces a less programmatic and more realistic plan for the set of essays that comprise Martin Warnke's book. The subject is 'The Art History of Nature'. The implication of the title as a whole is that nature, as an object of unmediated sensation, is unavailable for consultation. Lies, myths, fictions and theories are what we have instead. Warnke shows us how power and its representation are the stuff of our experience. There, of course, is something we would agree about at a *fin de siècle*. And at the end of a millenium, what would we not say about the imprisoning and enchaining effects of our arts?

However, it was not always like this: we look back to epochs when people believed that it was nature, not culture, that they contemplated. All the complications of the so-called postmodern perspective are present in Warnke's scholarly posture.

He tells us of our marking out of territory in concrete terms – sometimes in boundary markers of the most curious elaboration. Of course, since he is not a mythologist or a theoretical anthropologist, he does not tell us about Adam's aboriginal mark, as he delved and geometricized the Earth, and established 'mine and thine'.

Warnke tells us of the feudal age, when the castle stood on the hill. He describes the acquisition of land under its shadow, and the expropriation of political power. We might quibble at this point, and insist that land and power came together at an antecedent stage of our evolution. These stoney piles are prominent in our imagined history; but Adam Smith would have us believe, reasonably, that it was long before, when we ceased to live in a state of nature, that property and stock (the prime elements of political power) came into existence. There was a fence round a field and a store within the pale. As Robert Frost said, in the pure spirit of lapsarianism, 'Good fences make good neighbours.'

In other words, there are other accounts of our territory and its past to put alongside Warnke's. This is a problem for the seeker-after-truth. Indeed, the book under review lacks a certain virtue: it fails to circumscribe its topic and conduct the reader to its illuminated centre. However, in that, it also escapes a vice: it is not dogmatic. It is also a mine of strange information. Surely it is not common knowledge any more that the tweaking of children's ears activates their memories! (p.12)

The reader is in continuous debate with the text. Should Warnke not think on about the tyrant's castle? He describes it as a rural structure and he hints that the Duc de Berry, in the early 15th century, is the tyrannical occupant of the castles that dominate the landscapes illustrating the Labours of the Months in the *Très Riches Heures*. But that is a twentieth century reading, one contradicting the message of feudal reciprocity that the imagery intended to communicate. Art history – the study of what was meant and understood when works were made – periodically gives way to social history, when imagery is used as unwitting illustration of past conditions.

In truth, a rural tyrant is a poor example of the species. The true tyrant is a veritable dragon who wallows upon a huge mound of riches. He lives off a large population and, as the 15th century Italian architecural theorist, Alberti says, he builds his castle in threatening propinquity to the town. By the same token, the tower houses of Scotland, if they spoke of the domination of revolting peasants, were, in their isolation, the dwellings of, at best or worst, parochial tyrants.

The landscape that Warnke studies is, again and again through his book, shaped by conflict, and the peace that it might declare is frequently the peace of victory rather than armistice. He includes a fascinating history of the colossus, the attempt to make ineradicable the image of the victor in the landscape. Here is a case where the landscape of fact and of art intend to be indistinguishable. As has already been suggested, Warnke sometimes fails to make the distinction in his own text. On one occasion, he denounces a painting for failing to acknowledge contemporary developments in warfare. But this is to get things the wrong way round. It is unsatisfactory to return from a discussion of warfare in the 17th century to a battle picture by Rubens, and dismiss the latter as a matter of 'wishful thinking' (because the battle is conducted by heroes rather than a nameless soldiery). Rubens painted realities – the *realpolitik* of absolutism. As a student of the *Art History of Nature*, Warnke should take care to acknowledge purpose and meaning. He should be slower to find misrepresentation.

His book stimulates argument again. Looking principally at the German landscape and German art, he has little to say about the Scottish landscape. However, both have such a crucial place in the making of Romantic landscape, that to see examples of German landscape art is, for most poetical purposes, to see Scotland through 19th century eyes. If vision is to some extent a matter of cultural inheritance, we are permitted to guess at how, shaped in the mould of Romantic vision, our more immediate forbears saw their world. Warnke's offers instruction in this. At his prompting, it is possible to ponder the landscape left behind (literally or in imagination) by the dead of the First World War. He writes movingly about Europe's soldiery's assumption of the colour of mud for the trenches of Passchaendael. What did Scottish soldiers make of the spectacle? Of course, they came mostly out of the cities and towns of Scotland. But was there a folk memory of the abandoned landscape of their Highland past? Surely, the landscape of the Somme can only have seemed like an argument about ownership when they saw the blasted shells of habitations. The blasted trees perhaps told of a different tragedy for the 'Enlightened'. If it was barbarism not to have the foresight to plant something of greater longevity that a human life, it was barbaric to unmake the landscape that had been husbanded by the contemporaries of Rubens. At the same time, we are prompted to note that ownership and disguise – or camouflage – replace the squaddies' duds today. It is troubling that green wellies are socially so conspicuous when they are visually so harmonized with their myre.

Politics is inseparable from ownership where landscape is concerned. There is, though, a tradition of landscape painting within which the challenge is to picture an *unowned* land. The thought was alive to an inspiring degree for the greatest of landscape painters, Claude Lorraine (1600-1682). If ownership could be removed from the scene, we will escape our utilitarian perspective. Then, we shall encounter ghosts and spirits and the very principles of nature. It were well for the reader of Warnke's book to keep this other landscape in mind.

Claude's proposition (in fact, a general cultural project) became an argument for the painters of Romantic Landscape: the aim was to journey to the very limit of civilized existence – which had expropriated the landscape in fact and imagination (as it had formed the city, the factory and the institution). Karl Carus (1789-1869) proclaimed this kind of landscape painting the primary *genre*, supplanting History Painting – the art of the death of kings. Caspar David Friedrich (1774-1840) painted landscape. The art of the death of the individual tells, at the same time, of where we might go and where we must stay. The individual is a self-indulgent fantasist who denies the *polis*. At the same time, he is the undead who feels no compunction to do so. The political landscape which Warnke's discusses, as he would no doubt readily acknowledge, does not subsume all the other landscapes which we inhabit. But it is an important one – one that we should not overlook.

This has been a provoking book – precipitate in its ideology and careless in its art-historical interpretation, often enough. But, just as I am not inclined to criticize Uncle Toby – another student of warfare – I am far from inclined to damn Warnke. A hobby-horse is as sensible a mode of transport as any in these postmodern times. Here, it is ridden with some *élan*. Warnke's book which, incidentally, is filled with a multitude of illustrations that would be useful for all sorts of other argumentative purposes, does not silence the reader. Instead, it stimulates question and discussion. I should like to read his analysis of 'Scott's View'.

The Hurt World: Short Stories of the Troubles
Michael Parker (ed.)
The Blackstaff Press, 1995
ISBN 0-85640-557-4 £12.99

Voices from a Far Country
Hugh Carr
The Blackstaff Press, 1995
ISBN 0-85640-545-0

JOHN HERDMAN

IT is not to be wondered at that contemporary writing from Northern Ireland should be dominated by the devastating impact of the Troubles; but are they a necessary defining ingredient? Michael Parker seems to be unsure, speaking of 'the point that "Troubles literature" – or rather, contemporary Northern Irish writing – is not just concerned with bombs and bullets, but with many other issues of power.' That could imply either that the alternative phrases in question are regarded as essentially synonymous, or that this collection is not precisely what it claims to be. Again, we might ask whether human concerns other than 'issues of power' are considered by the editor to have a place of any importance in this literature.

In fact, *The Hurt World* contains a few stories that are about are the Troubles, contemporary or historical, but are not from the North, and also others that are from the North but are not concerned with the Troubles, except as unstated background; and that is as it should be. The central question remains, how can events of overwhelming violence and horror be confronted and subdued by the writer in such a way that they yield a meaning and evoke a response that are different from, and deeper than, their impact as mere brute fact? How can the obdurate enormity of this material be transcended and transformed by art?

Frank O'Connor showed in his classic 'Guests of the Nation', which opens this volume, how an ultimate moral question can be posed with profound simplicity in a few highly charged pages. It is not to be expected that this can be done repeatedly. The most successful of the 21 stories in this collection achieve their effects through stark unadorned intensity, or laconic irony, or by adopting a variety of more complex, tangential approaches. Bernard MacLaverty's 'Walking the Dog', about the reactions of a totally uninvolved bystander who knows he may be about to become a casualty, grips the reader by the throat and enforces empathy. David Park's 'Killing a Brit' chillingly evokes the moral anaesthesia with which the familiarity of death and violence infects a child; while his 'Oranges from Spain' patiently builds up a picture of the complex humanity of the victim of a random shooting. Anne Devlin's 'Naming the Names' enters with insight into the conscience of a girl whose involvement in terrorism impels her to lead her lover to his death.

Some of the most interesting stories analyse the human implications of the Troubles from unfamiliar perspectives. William Trevor's sensitive 'The Distant Past' deals poignantly with the progressive isolation of an elderly brother and sister, survivors from the former Ascendancy in the north of the Republic. In the intensely imagined 'Green Roads', Maurice Leitch shows how the conscience of a British Army corporal who has committed a gratuitous act of violence on an innocent Irishman in England pursues him on his return to Ireland and convinces him of his coming doom: Leitch successfully marries realistic observation with a supernatural *frisson*. But perhaps the most psychologically compelling tale is 'Beatrice', in which Shane Connaughton explores, through the eyes of the man's young son, the complexities of the power nexus in the relationship between a police sergeant and the old lady from the Big House. Smarting from the hurts of history, the sergeant deliberately fells the woman's favourite tree, knowing that her dependence on his protection has now reversed their established roles.

The literary mode least equipped to transform this oppressive weight of lived experience is flat contemporary urban realism. An effective story has to be something more than an undistinguished sociology lecture in narrative form. 'Many of the stories,' writes the editor, 'exhibit their female characters' increasing impatience with, and resistance to, male readings and patriarchal order'. It has to be said that the stories which answer to this formula (not all of them written by women) are the dreariest and least rewarding in the volume.

Just across the border but a strangely different world: the 'far country' of Hugh Carr's novel is childhood and the 'voices' those of the people of the small town of Glengreeny in the Donegal of the 1940s, a slowly dying community with four pubs, six groceries and thirteen private houses. Conor O'Donnell is growing up in a 'kitchen bar' with Mama who is 'high strung', quarrels with everyone and makes her husband's life a misery, kind Dada who will never quite succeed in making a success of anything, and younger sister Betty. As with Joyce's *Portrait*, the narrative articulates itself through the slowly unfolding consciousness of a child, but its focus is directed not within, to delineate the mind of the artist, but outwards, to recreate and memorialise the vanished soul of the community through a rich and vivid accumulation of incidents, anecdotes, memories, impressions.

The novel has no chapters or clear linear progression: as Conor's discrete and shifting memories pile up and rub shoulders in a way that at first seems haphazard, a complex patchwork is formed in which hidden patterns develop and are seen gradually to emerge. Only slowly, too, does the reader come to realise with what care and skill each thread has been woven into this coat of many colours which is also a finished and shapely whole. For Conor does not rationalise; he observes and absorbs. A bit of a dreamer who remains slightly apart even as an ordinary boy among his ordinary friends, he woos his unattainable object of desire, Aisling the schoolmaster's daughter, not with words but with the music of his fiddle, as he hides behind the curtain. His memories, too, are like a musical composition in which themes announce themselves, disappear underground and resurface, variations are rehearsed, notes resonate and fade and are heard once more, subtly altered.

One recurrent *motif* is the 'emigrant tide', symbolised by the people's ambiguous relation to America – 'beyond' – an emblem of hope for the individual and of communal despair. Those who escape and make good leave behind, like Mama's first love, sadness and a nagging sense of loss; those who, like Conor's father, are repeatedly drawn back to Ireland by the umbilical cord which they cannot sever, smart under the reproach of failure. For Glengreeny as a whole America has the elusive reality of a dream, like the island far up the river which Conor and his friends never quite manage to attain: 'At least we saw the Island even if we didn't reach it. We can always come back another day.'

But the most insistent fact of life in Glengreen is death. There is nothing self-consciously elegiac about the treatment, though individual death clearly reflects the slow death of the community: it simply happens, to men and animals alike, and cannot be ignored. Hannah dies of old age, Sally Groarty in childbirth. Francey Dubh is killed in a lorry accident, oddball Willoughby, who believes himself pursued by old Nick, perishes in his blazing house, Crusoe kills himself to escape the ravages of his neglected cancer. Aisling's brother Ferdia, personification of hope and youthful vigour, succumbs to the complications of polio. And to death is added decay: Ned Mary the publican is carted off to the asylum, Suzanne to sad senility in the county home. Glengreeny's fecundity is all in the past, it seems: of birth we hear little.

The melancholy inherent in its subject-matter is more than offset, however, by the resonance and vitality of this novel's language, and by its wry, pointed humour. Hugh Carr has a superb ear, and a matchless resource in the vigour and idiosyncratic expressiveness of Donegal speech. If the dialogue is one of the book's chief glories, there is a sureness of touch and an evocative authority in every facet of the writing. Haven't we all heard 'winter scurrying like a rat across the slates'? Hugh Carr may be a first novelist, but he is clearly a highly seasoned writer.

Whither Marxism?: Global Crises in International Perspective
Bernd Magnus and Stephen Cullenberg (eds.)
Routledge, 1995
ISBN 0-415-91043-9 £12.99 pb

WILLY MALEY

Conference proceedings make for awkward publications. At their best, they bring together a coherent set of arguments on a common theme. At their worst, they offer a garbled collection of ideas, each essay aimed at a specialist audience, leading to low sales and lots of xeroxing. Either way, they call for a descriptive rather than a discursive review.

The companion volume to Jacques Derrida's monumental *Specters of Marx*, *Whither Marxism?* grew out of an international colloquium held at the Center for Ideas and Society at the University of California from 22-24 April 1993, and can be seen to be part of what Derek Mahon called in his 'Joycentenary Ode' a 'gineral Californication' of culture and politics. Asked recently what the state of theory was, Derrida archly answered 'California', so it's no surprise that the state of Marxism should be deliberated there.

Those familiar with a collection of essays published in 1971, edited by Duncan Glen, entitled *Whither Scotland?*, will have a feeling of déjà vu reading this book. This volume has the same constituency of being an odd mixture of post-mortem and prophecy. The volume opens with some questions: 'Has the collapse of communism spelled the death of Marxism and of Marx as an important political thinker? Given the plight of the homeless, the lack of adequate health care, environmental degradation, racism, and enormous national debt burdens, what sort of model for the future do we have? What is the status of Marxist social goals such as the egalitarian distribution of income, increased workplace democracy, the end of economic exploitation and the eradication of class differences?'

The ten essays that grapple with those questions are divided into two parts. In Part One, 'Marxism's Future?'. In 'The Obsolescence of Marxism?', Douglas Kellner sets the tone of the collection when he asserts that 'just as Marxist critics too quickly proclaimed the demise of capitalism, so too have critics of Marxism too glibly forecast its death'. Kellner then proceeds to separate what is living and what is dead in Marxism, seeking to rescue theory from praxis, and thus falling into the trap that Derrida foresaw of retrieving an academic Marx at the expense of a political one.

Abdul Janmohamed, in 'Refiguring Values, power, knowledge: or Foucault's Disavowal of Marx', claims that, despite his constant denial, resistance, and rejection of Marxist thought, the work of the French philosopher Michel Foucault betrays an indebtedness to Marx, and belongs to a Western 'culturalist' or super-structuralist tradition that postpones the politico-economic till the last instance. Thus Foucault, like Kellner, wards off questions of economy in order to focus upon discursive formations.

'Marxism from Scientific to Utopian', by Zhang Longxi, reverses Engels' opposition in *Socialism: Utopian and Scientific*, and, in a move that mirrors Derrida's charged advocacy of the messianic demand for justice in Marx, underlines the importance of the utopian strand in socialist thought, attacking Engels's naive faith in science: 'The unabashed scientism in Engels's book, the confidence in the objective laws of nature and society, the teleology of history as the unfolding of historical necessity beyond human will and consciousness, all these become highly suspect in a world of post-Hegelian philosophy and post-World War II politics'. Zhang contends that the shell of scientism can be shed in favour of a kernel of revolutionary desire: 'Indeed, when communism has collapsed in the East, when what went on in the name of Marx and his political theory has proved to be disastrous and repressive, it is the utopian vision, the desire and hope for a more authentically human society, more than any "scientific" approach designed to reach that land of prophecy through class struggle and the dictatorship of the proletariat, that may yet sustain our interest in Marxism and command our respect for Karl Marx as one of the great visionaries of human history'.

The starting-point of Andrei

Marga's 'The Modern World and the Individual' is the reality of Marxism in present-day Eastern Europe. 'After holding a monopoly on intellectual life, being for many years a compulsory subject in universities, and being spread through official propaganda, Marxism is buried in oblivion and, actually, dispatched to the museum'. The rest of the article is taken up by an investigation of Marxism, which concludes that a new anthropology is called for, and a new humanism which, while drawing on some of the insights of Marxism, will reject its programmatic militancy: 'Rather, a Marxism reconstructed at the level of present experience would be a distant follower of Marx, the result of complicated marriages, which could no longer justify the name of Marxism'.

In 'Supplementing Marxism', the only essay in the volume by a woman – a revealing comment on Marxism and gender – and the only one to draw explicitly on 'Queer Theory', Gayatri Chakravorty Spivak anticipates Derrida's claim that 'socialism is about justice, not primarily about development'. Spivak's essay, dense and telegraphic, is further proof that the literary critics are the best readers of Marx.

Part Two, 'Transition to/from Socialism', opens with Carlos Vilas' 'Forward Back: Capitalist Restructuring, the State and the Working Class in Latin America', which suggests that the apparent retreat of the state in Latin America – which manifests itself in 'a slimmer public sector' – is merely a displacement of the state, as the strings of the economy are pulled from elsewhere. The suggestion that Latin America is entering a post-state stage is thus premature. This recalls the Big Government versus Small Government debates of the past where Big Government meant welfare and Small Government meant a big stick and a big army. Vilas's conclusion points to the specificity of the Latin American experience: 'The European and Central Asian breakdown of Soviet-type political regimes, which have never existed in Latin America – short of the Cuban case – or of Marxist-Leninist thinking, which was much more important in left-wing academic circles than in Latin American politics, pose no particular questions in terms of an alleged exhaustion of critical paradigms. On the contrary, they free the creative quest for people's political and social alternatives from the Manichean dialectics of the Cold War'.

Following on from Vilas, Keith Griffin and Azizur Rahman Khan argue, in 'The Transition to Market Guided Economies: Lessons for Russia and Eastern Europe from the Chinese Experience', explore the process of economic reform begun in 1978, and caution that 'the Chinese experience underlines the necessity to create an effective social safety net to protect those who are harmed during the transition to a market-guided economy'. The authors do not give due consideration to the fact that the market and social safety are not entirely compatible.

Ashot Galoian's 'Marxism, the Nationality Question and Soviet Leadership: A Comparative Discussion of Western Views and Political Reality' is one of the most incisive and relevant essays in the volume. Galoian, a Professor of Political History in the Republic of Armenia, argues that nationalism was the driving force both behind the break-up of the Soviet Union, and the Russian Revolution itself, and does so with a wealth of detail on the complex dialectic between class and nation in twentieth-century Marxism.

In 'Lessons from the USSR: Taking Marxian Theory the Next Step', Stephen Resnick and Richard Wolff contend that Marxism is 'the dialectical "other" of capitalism', and, again in keeping with Derrida's book on Marx, argue that Marxism is yet to come: 'The Marxist issue ... remains on the agenda now as it did in 1917. When, where, how, and why will a crisis of either state or private capitalism result not in a transition from one to the other but rather in a revolution to communism?'

The absence of an index gives the reader extra work, but this is a book that, with all its faults, offers a timely challenge to the premature pronouncements on the end of communism and the death of Marxism. There was an old saying in Eastern Europe: 'Under communism, the minorities dance'. Now that Marxism is fast becoming in the East the minority, dissident culture that it always was in the West, it may be time to learn some new steps. *Whither Marxism?*, with all its contradictions and inconsistencies, is an open invitation to dance.

SHORTLEET

Non-Person Singular
Selected Poems of Yang Lian
The Wellsweep Press, 1 Grove End House, 150 Highgate Rd, London
ISBN 0 948454 15 6 p/b 128pp. £7.95

Bilingual text featuring superb translations by Brian – Men o the Mossflow – Holton. Yang is one of the so-called 'misty' or 'ambiguist' poets who rose to prominence in China in the 1980's, where his work has been banned since 1983. He is now exiled in Germany, where he continues his work bridging Chinese tradition to western modernism. The scope of his creative imagination is astounding, and this, allied to his ability to capture an image or a mood in a few brief words, suggests that Yang Lian is one of the great world poets of our era. Every poem bristles with an urgent energy, transcending characteristically bleak subject matter, and brilliantly captured in Holton's English versions. Wellsweep are to be congratulated in bringing his work to an English speaking audience. This is not merely a recommended publication but an essential one.

War
Klaus Rifberg
Fjord Press, PO Box 16349, Seattle, WA 98116
ISBN 0 940242 66 4 p/b 69pp. $10.00

Rifberg is Denmark's foremost contemporary poet and this volume contains an ambitious long poem made up of a series of smaller untitled pieces, originally published in 1992 and translated here by Steven T. Murray and Tiina Nunnally. War describes how those people who are distanced from the actuality of conflict are drawn into vicarious voyeuristic involvement through media coverage, acquiescent of its existence as long as it doesn't happen to them, even praying for the destruction of a kind of necessary catharsis. Descriptions of daily life contrast with italicised commentary on the coming of the unspecified *krigen*, which slowly builds until the spectre of death hovers over this powerful work like a stealth bomber, suggesting that we are all guilty of turning up at the arena to watch the innocent slain, and giving another meaning to the term 'Gulf War syndrome'.

Transitions 1: Writing from the European borderlands
ed. Hildi Hawkins and Radojka Miljevic
19 Queen Court, Queen Square, London WC1N 3BB
ISBN 0 903425 90 4 135pp. £6.95

First of a new half-yearly anthology, featuring poetry and prose from eastern Europe. This issue contains work by Gösta Ågrel, Karel Matej Capek-Chod, Péter Esterhazy, Jaan Kaplinski, Igor Klikovac, Leena Krohn, Ivan V.

Lalic, Viivi Luik, Bornislaw Maj, Dusan Mitana and Dubravka Ugresic, and varies between a northern journey through the Finnish archipelago by Ågrel, to meditations on life during wartime by Sarajevo-based Klikovac and Croatian Ugresic. *Transitions* features some of the best translators in their fields and is a handsome production which deserves to succeed. Subscription costs £15.00 for two issues.

Harvesting the Edge
G. F. Dutton
The Menard Press, 8 The Oaks, Woodside Ave, London N12 8AR
ISBN 1 874320 01 2 p/b £8.99

Subtitled 'some personal explorations from a marginal garden', this book shows how Dutton's skills – scientist of international repute, mountaineer and wild water swimmer, award winning poet – interface with nature in his Highland garden. A series of seven essays describe the seasons in a mutually informative play of prose and poetry. At the core of this book is Geddesian philosophy applied; 'you interfere only when you have to, and with least disturbance, you learn to study the life of plant and animal, ally and competitor; you realise your human responsibility and power of compassion, on this vigorous battlefield; how to carry safely and use to the minimum, your saw, snare and gun or your new chemical weapons, which are so crude compared with the delicately murderous molecular armoury concealed about you in fiercely rivalsome root, leaf and blossom. You begin to understand why good design grows from this knowledge...'

Talking Verse: Interviews with Poets
ed. Crawford, Hart, Kinloch, Price
Verse, University of St. Andrews, KY16 9AL
ISBN 1 872612 05 9 p/b 229 pp. £10

A volume of interviews with poets taken from ten years of the now sadly defunct poetry magazine, including amongst others Adcock, Armitage, Burnside, Harrison, Jamie, Kuppner, Leonard, Morgan, Murray, O'Brien and Sweeney. A valuable record of its time, this publication is highly recommended to those with an interest in contemporary poetry in Scotland and beyond, ranging broadly through discussion of the creative process as the individual experiences it, and including many insights into the influences and backgrounds of the poets featured. Robert Crawford's introduction outlines the magazine's origins and aims.

Last Things First/Na rudan deireannach air thoiseach
New Writing Scotland 13
ed. A. L. Kennedy, James McGonigal, Meg Bateman
ASLS, University of Aberdeen, AB9 2UB
ISBN 0 948877 27 8 p/b 162pp. £6.95

Over fifty writers are featured in *NWS13*, which demonstrates the renewed interest in Gaelic language work and in particular, Gaelic prose. In the introduction, the editors identify a thread running through the submissions concerned with the 'four last things... death, judgement, heaven or hell,' and wonder if this reflects the current concerns of the population in a time of 'political endings and beginnings, an increasing insecurity at local and international level, personal loss or gain.' As might be expected from this broad rubric, there is a great breadth of subject and style contained here and the diversity of work is further evidence of the richness of contemporary literature in Scotland. Writers are presented alphabetically by surname, making this a volume to dip at random into rather than read for connections between juxtaposed pieces, and the number of new or unfamiliar names really does justify the 'new writing' *sluagh-ghairm*.

Medusa Dozen and other poems
Tessa Ransford
The Ramsay Head Press, 15 Gloucester Place, Edinburgh
ISBN 1 873921 03 9 p/b £6.50

The title sequence of thirteen poems is a meditation upon the feminine, which slides easily between the voice of myth, the serpent-goddess, and woman particular, setting up a dialectic for the examination of the gulf between women and men. Ransford's technique is sublime, able to characterise conflict and harmony without obtruding into the reader's awareness, as she makes for an understanding of the woman in herself, for herself, rather than defined in the negative as not man – a point made perfectly in the following lines: 'some are great and some/have greatness thrust/ (like Samson's hairy head)/ into their lap.' Elsewhere in this volume, Ransford's concerns are with her own Indian childhood, as in the section 'Exchange of Dreams', with Scottish margins in 'Rough Bounds' and with poetry itself. Throughout her voice is firm and true to itself.

Collected Poems
Flora Garry
Gordon Wright Publishing, 25 Mayfield Road, Edinburgh EH9 2NQ
ISBN 0 903065 82 7 p/b £7.95

Poems in her native 'Buchan dialect' and in English are presented here, along with two short prose pieces and a number of photographs of the author – now in her nineties and still as beautiful as she obviously was when a girl. Her Scots writing has a native density that is likely to be envied by younger Scots poets forced to turn to the dictionary for similar freshness of expression. On the evidence of this slim volume it is to be regretted that she has written no more, for these are finely wrought pieces without exception. Perhaps she has suffered from lack of encouragement in the past, like some other Scottish women writers of her generation. If so, then this publication should go some way towards compensating for that wrong.

Horridge
Hugh McMillan
Chapman Publishing, 4 Broughton Place, Edinburgh EH1 3RX
ISBN 0 906772 52 4 p/b 62pp £5.95

McMillan's third collection confirms that behind his sardonic wit, an insensitive poetic nature lurks – a quirky cleverness that skips across the undulations of form and pattern to actually entertain. But why paraphrase when McMillan can illustrate in as many words, viz:

> **A Scottish Hoy-You**
> (A Hoy-You is an ancient Scottish verse form of 3 lines and 15 syllables, traditionally written by people who have nothing to say and addressed to those who don't want to hear it. The 1990's seems a particularly favourable context in which to reinvent this classical form.)
>   Here's tae us, wha's
>   like us? Damn few an they're aa
>   on tea towels.

Great stuff and worth every syllable.

At The Aviary
Stewart Conn
Snailpress, 30 Firfield Road, Plumstead 7800, South Africa
ISBN 1 874923 21 3 32pp p.o.a.

Eighteen poems arising out of two visits to South Africa made by Conn, in 1984 and 1993, which taken together amount to a traveller's sketchbook, capturing the essence of the experience. Conn's skill at transforming the language of everyday experience into a tightly compacted poetic vehicle is exemplary, just as he seems able to extract from situations those images which most resonate with symbolic significance.

Herts Bluid
David Purves
Chapman Publishing, 4 Broughton Place, Edinburgh EH1 3RH
ISBN 0 906772 70 2 p/b £5.95

A first collection of poetry in Scots by the editor of *Lallans* and long-time champion of the language. Purves is Selkirk-born, but his writing makes use of the breadth of linguistic variation from area to area of Scotland, although as might be expected Purves has established his own strict orthographic convention. His poems are marked by a tension between a tendency towards the homiletic that is resistent of a gentler lyricism – which nevertheless pokes through, generally with an exclamation mark to pinpoint the irony.

The Return of Burke and Hare
Raymond Burke
Dualchas, 1/R, 21 Garturk St, Glasgow
ISBN 0 9521418 3 3 p/p 158pp. £4.99

Script of the musical comedy play which updated the Burke and Hare story to the present day, with a message of concern over the state of the NHS. The book is introduced by Owen Dudley Edwards, who writes that this is 'a work of fine wit, song and pace, and a masterly plucking of comedy from the heart of tragedy.' Music for the play's seven songs follows the script itself.

An Old Man Dances in George Square
Maryhill Writers Group
Smeddum Press, c/o Maryhill Burgh Halls, Garbraid Ave, Glasgow
ISBN 0 9523868 52 p/b 64pp. £2.00

A mixed collection of poetry and prose from thirteen members of the writers group and a poem from tutor Agnes Owens. An ironic vein of defiant protest runs through the work, neatly illustrated by the closing verse of Tommy Orr's 'The B-Attitudes: Blessed are the meek/ for they shall inheret the earth/Poor bastards!/ Fucked again!' Introduced by James Kelman, this auld man's dance is worth a couplae quid o anybody's money.

Three Monologues
Jennifer Johnston
Lagan Press, PO Box 110, Belfast BT12 4AB
ISBN 1 873687 70 2 p/b 68pp. £4.95

Three beautifully constructed narratives by one of Ireland's outstanding writers, capturing perfectly the casual intimacy of secrets shared between old friends, but charged with the energy of religious war. In *Twinkletoes*, Karen, a top IRA prisoner's wife, tries to come to terms with the difference between the loneliness of her life and the respected position she holds in her community, while the other two monologues *Musn't Forget High Noon* and *Christine* present the viewpoints of a husband and wife. In the former, Billy Maltseed, a border Protestant, reflects on the death of a friend, while the latter shows his wife in mourning, after Billy's violent death. Funny and terrible by turns.

SCOTTISH Affairs

Scottish Affairs is the definitive forum for comment a debate on Scottish politics, society and current affairs. It published in book form every quarter. It is independent political parties and pressure groups.

Issue no. 15 (April 1996) includes articles on:

A Sustainable Scotland
Local Government and Economic Development
The Scottish Constitutional Convention
Language and Identity

Annual subscription (four issues):
£25 (individuals), £40 (institutions)

Published by:

Unit for the Study of Government in Scotland,
Chisholm House,
High School Yards,
Edinburgh.
EH1 1LZ
Tel: 0131 650 2456
Fax: 0131 650 6345

Edinburgh Review

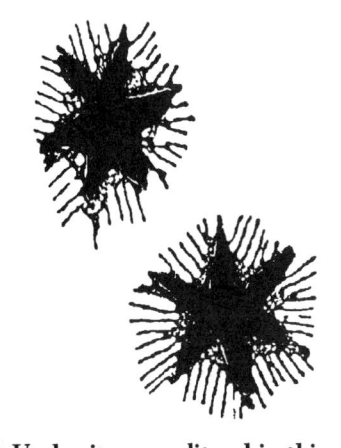

Under its new editorship this acclaimed literary and cultural review will continue to publish a wide range of original and topical material with a new emphasis on the literary by both new and established writers. Lively, controversial and eclectic, **Edinburgh Review** is the only forum which positively asserts the rich diversity of Scottish arts and culture while attending to international literary and cultural events. New poetry and short stories rub shoulders with philosophical musings, interviews and book reviews in 'Scotland's **foremost intellectual/ literary magazine'.**
Scotland on Sunday.

1996 SUBSCRIPTION RATES (2 Issues)
2 issues a year - Winter and Summer
ISSN 0267-6672

Individuals		**Institutions**	
UK and EC	£15	UK and EC	£30
Overseas	£16.50	Overseas	£33
N. America	$29.50	N. America	$59.50

Postage
Surface postage included in the subscription.
Please add £5 or $10 for airmail delivery.

HOW TO ORDER
Return this form to:
Journals Marketing Dept
EDINBURGH UNIVERSITY PRESS LTD
22 George Square
Edinburgh EH8 9LF
Tel: 0131 650 6207/Fax: 0131 662 0053

☐ Please send me a 2 issue subscription to *Edinburgh Review*.

NAME _____

ADDRESS _____

_____ POSTCODE _____

☐ I enclose cheque/money order
(made payable to Edinburgh University Press)

☐ Please debit my VISA/Mastercard

Account number

_____

Expiry date _____

Scotlands

The Journal of Scottish Culture

Scotlands seeks to be enlightening and comprehensive, featuring fresh academic work on a wide range of subjects. Each issue will contain essays from leading scholars in the arts, literature, music, history and current affairs.

SUBSCRIPTION RATES
Volume 3, 1996   ISSN 1350-7508
Two issues a year - Winter and Summer

Individuals		**Institutions**	
UK and EC	£20	UK and EC	£35
Overseas	£22	Overseas	£38
N. America	$38.50	N. America	$65

HOW TO ORDER
Return this form with your payment to:
Kathryn MacLean, Journals Dept, Edinburgh University Press Ltd,
22 George Square, Edinburgh EH8 9LF, Fax: 0131 662 0053

☐ Please enter my subscription to *Scotlands*, Volume 3, 1996

☐ I am interested in subscribing to *Scotlands*, please send me a free sample copy.

☐ I enclose a cheque (made payable to Edinburgh University Press Ltd)

☐ Please debit my VISA/Mastercard - Account no._____
Expiry date

Name_____

Address_____

Postcode_____   Country_____